THE LAST YEARS OF
WEST MIDLANDS
STEAM

PETER TUFFREY

FOREWORD BY PETE WATERMAN

GREAT NORTHERN

ACKNOWLEDGEMENTS

I would like to thank the following people for their help: Roger Arnold, Ben Brooksbank, David Burrill, John Chalcraft, Paul Chancellor, David Christie, John Clayson, Peter Crangle, David Joy, John Law, Hugh Parkin, Richard Postill, Bill Reed, John Ryan, Andrew, Rachel and Sue Warnes, Pete Waterman, Bill Wright.

Gratitude should also be expressed to my son Tristram for his general help and encouragement throughout the course of the project.

Great Northern Books
PO Box 1380, Bradford, BD5 5FB
www.greatnorthernbooks.co.uk

ISBN: 978-1-914227-01-1

Design and layout: David Burrill

CIP Data
A catalogue for this book is available from the British Library

FOREWORD

PETE WATERMAN

I was born at the end of the Second World War in the Midlands. The area never seemed to be magical, but looking back I was so lucky you could say lucky lucky. Although it was bleak, there was a magic, a romance that I felt so strongly.

I started 'spotting' early. Well, to be honest, I'm not sure it was 'spotting', more like making railway journeys where looking out of the window kept me quiet. Rugby was visited every Wednesday and Leamington Spa on Tuesdays, so my mum could see her sisters. At Rugby, with its gloomy surroundings, steam-breathing monsters burst into the station with all the power of fire-eating dragons. I still see those blue engines as if it were yesterday. Leamington Spa was the opposite, as the engines looked neater, with the copper and the brass shining and their names providing even more romance. The sight of my first 'Hall' in mixed traffic black, with red name plates, made me an immediate devotee of the Western Region. These magical encounters with the railways have stayed with me all my life.

Railways of the West Midlands were all I cared about at weekends and during school holidays. All my free time was spent 'spotting' and there was nothing I loved more than to be in some dirty railway location without a care in the world. The first lyrics I ever wrote – long before I thought of music as a career – were about the station at Rugby. To me, the hours sitting on a Saturday afternoon in the loneliness of Wolverhampton Stafford Road, with nothing but the smell of the railway, was all I wanted.

When music started to take over my life, I visited every place that my money would allow. Most trips were on my own as I had no mates that shared the passion I felt for the railways. Yes, some collected numbers and knew far more than me about the technical side, but for me it was the atmosphere of the railway that had the most appeal. The numerous personalities making up the staff and, yes, even the dirt, wear and tear, thanks to years of neglect, created a heady brew that had me intoxicated.

The weekend rover tickets you could obtain were a godsend for me. One weekend at Shrewsbury, I put over eighty numbers in my book and, more importantly, I spent ten hours chasing a dream. This book is full of dreams for me. I had many hours at most of the places in my notebook – some more, others less. Saltley was easy to explore, whilst Aston proved almost impossible. I can smell my egg sandwiches in my duffel bag now as I look at these photographs and drift back to those distant days. I would always try and sit in the cab of a locomotive and eat them, pretending to be on the main line going at sixty miles an hour. In reality, I was in the cab of a dead 'Super D' in some dark shed, or in an overgrown scrap line.

Happy reading and please pass me an egg sandwich.

Pete Waterman.

INTRODUCTION

Covering some 5,000 square miles, the West Midlands was well-served by a variety of railway lines, ranging from main lines to branches, connecting routes and industrial systems. Before the massive reorganisation of British Railways in the 1950s and 1960s, the area was a bustling and vibrant place for enthusiasts to observe and record steam locomotives at work. In doing so, a lost era was captured and this collection has been assembled to celebrate those bygone days.

The West Midlands is comprised of the smaller West Midlands county (formed by the Local Government Act 1972), Herefordshire, Shropshire, Staffordshire, Warwickshire and Worcestershire. Several cities are in the area: Birmingham, Coventry, Hereford, Lichfield, Stoke-on-Trent, Wolverhampton and Worcester. There are also a number of large towns, such as: Burton-on-Trent, Dudley, Kidderminster, Leamington Spa, Nuneaton, Rugby, Shrewsbury, Stafford, Stourbridge, Tamworth, Uttoxeter, etc.

At several locations in the West Midlands, the Industrial Revolution was kindled in the late 18th century and this attracted several canal undertakings. With the success of early railways – the Stockton & Darlington and Liverpool & Manchester – lines were planned in the West Midlands. The Grand Junction Railway connected Birmingham with the Liverpool & Manchester Railway on opening in July 1837 and this was soon followed by the completion of the London & Birmingham Railway just over a year later. Several undertakings were spurred on as a result and these linked the area to both local and national rail networks.

From the smaller companies that promoted original lines in the West Midlands grew larger entities that dominated traffic. The London & North Western Railway was formed from the merger of the Grand Junction Railway and the London & Birmingham Railway, whilst the Midland Railway cut through thanks to the Birmingham & Derby Junction line and route from Birmingham to Gloucester. The Great Western Railway expanded into the area by purchasing several lines, which eventually provided the company with a main line from London to Birkenhead, via Birmingham and Wolverhampton, as well as a dominant position in the west with routes between Worcester, Kidderminster and Shrewsbury.

Whilst these larger companies dominated much

of the West Midlands, the North Staffordshire Railway was able to establish a foothold in the area around Stoke-on-Trent. Incredibly, this centre for pottery production had no rail connection when the NSR company was founded in 1845 to remedy this oversight. Several schemes had been brought together and in 1846 a line from Congleton to Stoke and Colwich on the Trent Valley Railway line (then operated by the LNWR) between Stafford and Rugby received authorisation. A second route was approved and this ran from North Rode (between Congleton and Macclesfield) to Burton-on-Trent via Uttoxeter. Alongside these main schemes were a number of branches, such as one to Crewe and Sandbach. Construction began in late 1846 and took around 18 months for the main lines, whilst most of the original system was operational in the early 1850s; later the company had 216 route miles. Though there were a number of proposals to take over the NSR, none came to fruition and the company was amalgamated with the LNWR, MR and several others to form the London, Midland & Scottish Railway at Grouping in 1923.

Through the 1920s and 1930s, the LMSR consolidated all lines under the company's control, including those in the West Midlands. Competition continued to be provided by the Great Western Railway, which saw a number of smaller companies amalgamated at Grouping. The GWR was perhaps using stronger locomotives at this time as the LMSR was disadvantaged by poor LNWR and MR designs right through to the early 1930s. At this time, W.A. Stanier became Chief Mechanical Engineer and introduced several standard classes that modernised the company's motive power and many remained in use under BR to the end of steam.

The railways were particularly affected by the hardships of the Second World War and these were still evident into the 1950s, with many sheds left in a dilapidated condition. Several locomotive classes also survived, when in other circumstances they would have been sent to the scrapyard. The 'Big Four' railway companies had been taken over by the government at the start of war, but this became Nationalisation in 1948, partly due to the investment necessary in the motive power and infrastructure. This was slow to materialise and the Modernisation Plan of 1955 was necessary to really make a difference. In the West

Midlands, this mainly concerned the electrification of the West Coast Main Line and the reconstruction of a number of stations, notably Birmingham New Street and Coventry.

Whilst investment and improvement of the railways in the late 1950s and early 1960s was hoped to change the fortunes of the industry, the biggest factor causing the problems was out of the control of BR. This was the rise of private transport, particularly haulage firms that took freight traffic away, causing a drastic fall in revenue and irreparable damage. Although steam had been scheduled for replacement by diesel locomotives, this was to be a gradual process until the financial situation seriously worsened and the timetable was sped up. By the mid-1960s, many steam engines were being withdrawn and those left in service appeared increasingly worn-out and dishevelled.

Further savings were thought to be possible by closing stations and unremunerative lines. In the south of the West Midlands area, the Evesham loop, which bypassed the notorious Lickey Incline, was partially abandoned, whilst the connection between Ashchurch, Tewkesbury and Great Malvern was severed. Similarly, the line from Worcester to Leominster was completely closed in 1964 and the track lifted. Though remaining open to freight traffic, the route from Water Orton to Walsall and Wolverhampton ceased to have scheduled passenger services in early 1965. With the completion of the electrification of the WCML, the ex-GWR line from Birmingham Snow Hill to Wolverhampton lost favour during the mid-1960s and services steadily declined to closure in the early 1970s. Yet, services have since returned and those to Moor Street station have dramatically improved following near-closure around the same time.

Whilst the main line railways served the wider distribution of goods around and out of the West Midlands, many industrial concerns in the area had private railways. These often employed 0-6-0ST shunters, as well as other types, to move raw materials and finished products around their sites. The coal industry also had a vast network of lines that was attended to by an army of small locomotives.

The motive power scene in the West Midlands was quite varied, if dominated by W.A. Stanier's standard LMSR engines and C. Collett's GWR types. The aforementioned mainly consisted of Class 5 and 'Jubilee' 4-6-0s, together with 8F Class 2-8-0s, not forgetting the 'Coronation' Class Pacifics leading the principal expresses through the area on the WCML. Supporting roles were found for classes such as Sir Henry Fowler's 'Patriot' and 'Royal Scot' 4-6-0s and H.G. Ivatt's Class 2MT 2-6-0 and 2-6-2T Classes, as well as his Class 4MT 2-6-0. Also at work during the 1950s and 1960s were Beames/Cooke/Webb 0-8-0 Classes of the LNWR and MR 2F Johnson 0-6-0s and 3F 0-6-0Ts.

Collett's 4-6-0s dominated the ex-GWR main lines expresses, with 'Castle', 'Hall' and 'King' Classes prominent, with the mixed traffic 'Grange' and 'Manor' Classes on secondary services. Freight trains were handled by G.J. Churchward's 2800 Class 2-8-0s and the Collett variant 2884 Class, along with 4300 Class 2-6-0s, 2251 Class 0-6-0s and the 5205 Class 2-8-0Ts. Local passenger services were often operated by 5101 Class 2-6-2Ts and a variety of 0-6-0PT – 5700 Class, 8750 Class, 7400 Class, etc – while branch trains were entrusted to 1400 Class 0-4-2Ts.

During the early 1950s, BR's Standard Classes began entering service and several variants were to be found at work in the West Midlands. The Standard Class 7 'Britannia' Pacifics assisted the Stanier Pacifics and 4-6-0s on the WCML expresses, while secondary services had Standard Class 5 and 4 4-6-0s at the head. With the large amount of freight travelling in and around the area, Standard Class 9F 2-10-0s were a familiar sight.

The Last Years of West Midlands Steam celebrates the interesting post-Nationalisation period in the area up to the end of steam during the mid-1960s through evocative colour and black-and-white images. These have been taken at several of the major stations in the West Midlands, such as those in Birmingham, Wolverhampton, etc, as well as the numerous locomotive depots, both large and small, and the lineside – several shots capture engines hard at work on the notorious Lickey Incline. With these 'glory days' of steam now more than 50 years in the past, hopefully this collection serves to remind those youthful at the time of those wonderful years and spurs later generations into keeping them alive by supporting the several heritage lines subsequently established.

Peter Tuffrey
Doncaster, January 2021

Above ALDRIDGE STATION

The ex-London & North Western Railway 0-8-0s were coming to the end of their lives in 1964 and to commemorate the occasion the Stephenson Locomotive Society organised a tour of the Birmingham area. Taking place on 12th December, Beames G2 no. 49430 and Webb G2A no. 49361 hauled the train, which has made a stop at Aldridge station here. Photograph by Richard Postill.

Below ALVELEY COLLIERY

No. 1420 was in the midst of working a railtour in the Birmingham area with no. 4555 when pictured at Alveley Colliery on 19th September 1965. Photograph by Richard Postill.

Above ASHFORD BOWDLER

Between Ludlow and Leominster at Ashford Bowdler, Webb G2A 0-8-0 no. 49046 has a southbound freight in 1951. Photograph courtesy Rail Photoprints.

Below ASTON SHED

Stanier Class 5 4-6-0 no. 45000 is outside Aston shed, around 1960. Photograph courtesy Rail Photoprints.

ATHERSTONE
The 11.45am service from Liverpool to Rugby is at Atherstone station on 23rd May 1961. Stanier 'Jubilee' 4-6-0 no. 45737 *Atlas* is the motive power. Photograph by Hugh Ballantyne courtesy Rail Photoprints.

Above ASTON SHED

Stanier Class 5 no. 44685 has the motion oiled at Aston shed on 25th March 1964. The engine was allocated to Crewe North and survived until April 1967. Photograph by Richard Postill.

Below BADDESLEY COLLIERY

Beyer Garrett 0-4-0+0-4-0 no. 6841 *William Francis* is shunting wagons at Baddesley Colliery on 23rd September 1964. Employed there from new until withdrawal, the locomotive was subsequently preserved. Photograph by Neville Simms from the Ranwell Collection courtesy Rail Photoprints.

Above BARNT GREEN

A freight train is at Barnt Green with Ivatt Class 2MT 2-6-0 no. 46443 on 17th May 1963. Built at Crewe in February 1950, the locomotive was in traffic until March 1967. Photograph by Richard Postill.

Below BARNT GREEN

BR 9F no. 92127 approaches Barnt Green with a coal train on 17th May 1963. The engine was allocated to Wellingborough, though a move to Rowsley soon occurred. Photograph by Richard Postill.

Above BECKFORD STATION
On the Great Malvern to Evesham line, Beckford station was only open for a further three years when pictured on 15th October 1960. Photograph by B.W.L. Brooksbank.

Below BARNT GREEN STATION
Built by the Birmingham & Gloucester Railway in 1844, Barnt Green station later became an important junction with the Evesham loop in the 1850s. The station is pictured on 16th August 1963 with the loop platform on the left. Photograph by B.W.L. Brooksbank.

Above BESCOT SHED

With an important marshalling yard nearby, Bescot shed had a large complement of goods and freight locomotives. One of this contingent, Stanier 8F 2-8-0 no. 48726, is next to the depot's coaler on 11th August 1963. Photograph by Martyn Hunt courtesy Rail Photoprints.

Above BEWDLEY STATION

A quiet scene at Bewdley station on 16th August 1963. Dating from 1862, the station was on the Hartlebury-Shrewsbury line originally. Later, a connection was made with Tenbury, also the Shrewsbury & Hereford Railway, as well as a short extension being laid to Kidderminster. Bewdley managed to survive the Beeching cuts until 1970 when closed. Four years later, the station reopened as part of the Severn Valley Railway. Photograph by B.W.L. Brooksbank.

Opposite below BESCOT STATION

The Grand Junction Railway opened Bescot station as Bescot Bridge in 1837 following the completion of the line from Birmingham to Newton Junction with the Liverpool & Manchester Railway. From 1850, the station was Bescot Junction after trains began running to Walsall, though this had been dropped by the turn of the century. A further name change occurred on 16th August 1990 when Sir Stanley Matthews opened the station as Bescot Stadium, as Walsall Football Club had relocated a short distance away when a new stadium was built. Photograph by B.W.L. Brooksbank.

Above BESCOT SHED

Johnson 2F 0-6-0 no. 58277 is in the yard at Bescot shed on 24th March 1951. The locomotive was allocated to the depot and was withdrawn from there in November 1955. Photograph by B.W.L. Brooksbank.

Below BESCOT SHED

Stanier 2-6-0 no. 42975 is between duties at Bescot shed on 21st July 1963. A recent addition to the ranks, the engine was employed there until December 1964. Photograph by Richard Postill.

Above BILSTON CENTRAL STATION

Collett 'Castle' Class 4-6-0 no. 5000 *Launceston Castle* has the 11.05 Weymouth to Wolverhampton service at Bilston Central station on 25th July 1964. Photograph by Ian Turnbull courtesy Rail Photoprints.

Below BILSTON WEST STATION

Light engine at Bilston West station in 1965 is Collett '8750' 0-6-0PT no. 3650. Photograph by Brian Robbins courtesy Rail Photoprints.

Above BIRMINGHAM NEW STREET STATION

A wheel tapper appears to be checking the wheels of this cross country train before unrebuilt Fowler 'Patriot' Class 4-6-0 no. 45509 *The Derbyshire Yeomanry* departs from New Street station in 1957. Photograph courtesy Rail Photoprints.

Opposite above BIRMINGHAM NEW STREET STATION

Stanier Class 5 4-6-0 no. 44766 was built at Crewe Works in December 1947 as part of an order of 25. A number of these engines were part of a trial into the use of roller bearings, which were thought to reduce wear and increase time between maintenance visits to works. The first ten, including no. 44766, were fitted with Timken bearings on all the axles, whilst another ten used Skefko bearings on just the driving axle. Experience with both sets of engines justified the employment of roller bearings and this feature was subsequently adopted by British Railways for the Standard Classes. No. 44766 was also one of three Class 5s built at the time with a double chimney. Tests revealed no advantage to this application, although the engine remained with the apparatus until withdrawn; one of the trio did have the double chimney removed during the 1950s. No. 44766 is at Birmingham New Street station on 14th September 1963. Photograph by Richard Postill.

Opposite below BIRMINGHAM MOOR STREET STATION

Despite rebuilding Snow Hill station, the Great Western Railway still faced capacity problems in the early 20th century. The company decided a new station was necessary and this was to be dedicated to local traffic. Located a short distance away from Snow Hill to the south east, Moor Street station began serving passengers in 1909, though with temporary facilities and the buildings were not completed until 1914. This view shows the platforms on 5th September 1962 when in a run-down condition. Like many other stations, Moor Street suffered from declining local services in the 1950s and 1960s. Yet, the station did not close until the 1980s. A recent rise in commuter traffic led to a reopening in the early 2000s and a sympathetic restoration was later carried out. Photograph by B.W.L. Brooksbank.

Above BIRMINGHAM NEW STREET SOUTH TUNNEL

A train of empty stock – previously used for a Llandudno to Birmingham New Street express – emerges from New Street South tunnel on 7th August 1965. The photographer braved a wall topped with broken glass to capture this image from a point just off Moor Street, which also allowed sight of the ex-GWR lines to Moor Street station. This cutting is now covered by the Bull Ring development. Stanier Class 5 no. 45280 of Holyhead is leading the train. Photograph by B.W.L. Brooksbank.

Opposite above BIRMINGHAM NEW STREET STATION

Rebuilt Fowler 'Patriot' Class 4-6-0 no. 45531 *Sir Frederick Harrison* leaves Birmingham New Street station with an express for Euston on 23rd July 1948. The 'Patriot' Class was introduced in 1930 for express traffic and by 1934, 52 were in service. No. 45531 was built at Crewe Works in April 1933 as no. 6027, but was renumbered shortly after as no. 5531. The engine was nameless until 1937 when christened *Sir Frederick Harrison* after the General Manager of the LNWR at the turn of the century who had enjoyed a number of promotions from joining in 1864. No. 45531 was recently rebuilt with Stanier boiler, tender, etc, and is seen with British Railways experimental green livery. Photograph by B.W.L. Brooksbank.

Opposite below BIRMINGHAM NEW STREET STATION

Fowler 'Patriot' Class no. 45500 *Patriot* is at Birmingham New Street station with an express in April 1953. Allocated to Longsight shed, Manchester, at this time, the locomotive moved to Carlisle at the end of the year. Photograph courtesy Rail Photoprints.

BIRMINGHAM NEW STREET STATION

BR Standard Class 8 Pacific no. 71000 *Duke of Gloucester* has an express for Euston at New Street station on 20th May 1961. Photograph by Neville Simms from the Ranwell Collection courtesy Rail Photoprints.

Above and Below BIRMINGHAM NEW STREET STATION

As part of the West Coast Modernisation scheme of the early 1960s, Birmingham New Street station was completely rebuilt at a cost of £4.5 million. Here, some of the work has been captured. Above, the ex-LNWR (left) and ex-Midland Railway sections are seen and below, work on new platform roofs is viewed from Hill Street looking in the direction of Navigation Street. Both photographs by B.W.L. Brooksbank.

Above BIRMINGHAM SNOW HILL STATION

Passengers at Birmingham Snow Hill station prepare to board the 07.30 from Shrewsbury to Paddington on 26th April 1957. Collett 'King' Class 4-6-0 no. 6006 *King George I* is at the head of the train. Photograph by B.W.L. Brooksbank.

Opposite above BIRMINGHAM SNOW HILL STATION

No. 8109 was built at Swindon Works in February 1905 as part of G.J. Churchward's 3100 2-6-2T Class. Following some slight changes, the class was renumbered in the late 1920s to the 5100 Class. No. 8109 was originally no. 3115 and became no. 5115. Just over ten years later, the locomotive was rebuilt to become part of the 8100 Class and this meant larger driving wheels and an increase in boiler pressure. As no. 5115, the transformation occurred in November 1939, resulting in renumbering to 8109. The engine is ready to leave Birmingham Snow Hill station with a local service to Leamington Spa on 16th April 1963. Photograph by Neville Simms from the Ranwell Collection courtesy Rail Photoprints.

Opposite below BIRMINGHAM SNOW HILL STATION

View northward from the platform at Birmingham Snow Hill station to Hockley tunnel on 16th April 1963, as Collett 'Hall' Class 4-6-0 no. 4923 *Evenley Hall* takes the through line with an empty train of iron ore hopper wagons. Both ends of the station could prove challenging for heavy trains as gradients of 1 in 47 and 1 in 45 were present. Photograph by Neville Simms from the Ranwell Collection courtesy Rail Photoprints.

Above BIRMINGHAM SNOW HILL STATION

Although produced to work in South Wales on coal and freight trains, Collett's 5600 Class 0-6-2T locomotives later found work across the GWR system. Some 200 were built between 1924 and 1928, with no. 6683 appearing late on in October 1928. The engine has a freight train at Birmingham Snow Hill station on 3rd September 1962. Photograph by Richard Postill.

Opposite above BIRMINGHAM SNOW HILL STATION

Even though Churchward 'City' Class 4-4-0 no. 3440 *City of Truro* was possibly the first locomotive to reach 100 mph, the Great Western Railway did not intend to preserve the engine when withdrawn in March 1931. The Chief Mechanical Engineer of the company, Charles Collett, had to step in and no. 3440 was donated to the London & North Eastern Railway's museum at York. In 1957, the Western Region of BR returned *City of Truro* to steam and the engine worked various services through to 1962. No. 3440 has a Stephenson Locomotive Society special here on 25th August 1957 at Birmingham Snow Hill station. The train ran from the latter to the Southern Region's Eastleigh workshops, returning later in the day. Photograph courtesy Rail Photoprints.

Opposite below BIRMINGHAM SNOW HILL STATION

Collett 'Grange' Class 4-6-0 no. 6842 *Nunhold Grange* waits for the road at Birmingham Snow Hill station on 22nd August 1963. The engine was working from Stourbridge Junction shed at this time, though moved on to Tyseley before withdrawal in November 1964. Photograph by Richard Postill.

Above BIRMINGHAM SNOW HILL STATION
Hawksworth 'Modified Hall' Class 4-6-0 no. 7904 *Fountains Hall* pilots BR Standard Class 9F 2-10-0 no. 92001 through Birmingham Snow Hill station on 15th February 1964. Photograph by Richard Postill.

Opposite above BIRMINGHAM SNOW HILL STATION
On 25th August 1957, Churchward 2800 Class 2-8-0 no. 2833 leads a train of loaded hopper wagons through Birmingham Snow Hill station. The locomotive is passing North signal box which was installed in 1909 and had 224 levers to control movements at the north end of the station. Both no. 2833 and the signal box would be taken out of service at the end of the 1950s. Photograph courtesy Rail Photoprints.

Opposite below BLACKWELL STATION
Stanier Class 5 no. 44888 has just tackled the formidable Lickey incline with this express and has reached the summit at Blackwell in August 1957. The locomotive was built at Crewe Works in August 1945 and subsequently spent most of the 1950s at Saltley shed. Despite a large number of moves in the 1960s, no. 44888 managed to survive to the end of steam in August 1968. Photograph courtesy Rail Photoprints.

Above BRIDGNORTH STATION

On the Hartlebury to Shrewsbury line, Bridgnorth station opened to passengers in February 1862. This view was captured looking northward just over 100 years later on 24th April 1962 and little over a year remained before closure. Thankfully, the station later reopened as part of the Severn Valley Railway and is presently the northern terminus, with the workshops also located nearby. Photograph by B.W.L. Brooksbank.

Opposite above BLACKWELL STATION

The lack of adequate braking systems for much of the existence of the railways is highlighted by the sign on the left. Even in the 1960s, many wagons were still running without being fitted with brakes and runaway trains were possible with gradients as extreme as those on the Lickey Incline. Fowler 4F no. 44092 has tackled the bank in the opposite direction and has reached Blackwell station with a Class H freight in 1956. Saltley-allocated at this time, no. 44902 was later condemned at Newton Heath shed during April 1964. Photograph courtesy Rail Photoprints.

Opposite below BORDESLEY JUNCTION

A group of sidings were present just south east of Bordesley station on the GWR line to Birmingham Moor Street. A connection was made with the ex-Midland Railway line from Gloucester which passed over the GWR route between the station and the sidings and this was Bordesley Junction. Collett 'Grange' Class 4-6-0 no. 6859 *Yiewsley Grange* has been held by a signal and is just moving off with this freight train in 1957. Photograph courtesy Rail Photoprints.

Above BOURNVILLE
Johnson 1142 Class 0-6-0 no. 58143 is at Bournville in 1959. The locomotive was built in 1875 and managed to survive until November 1963. Photograph courtesy Rail Photoprints.

Below BLOXWICH STATION
View north to Bloxwich station on 15th April 1962. The station – on the line between Walsall and Rugeley – was open for a further three years, though a new facility was established further north in the late 1980s. Photograph by B.W.L. Brooksbank.

Above BRIERLEY HILL STATION
Opened in 1858 by the Oxford, Worcester & Wolverhampton Railway, Brierley Hill station closed in July 1962 and is pictured two months after that event. Photograph by B.W.L. Brooksbank.

Below BRIDGNORTH STATION
Churchward 4300 Class 2-6-0 no. 6388 has a train of empty coal wagons at Bridgnorth station on 30th December 1960, whilst Collett 6100 Class 2-6-2T no. 6128 is travelling northward with a freight service. Photograph by Hugh Ballantyne courtesy Rail Photoprints.

BROMSGROVE STATION

Two Stanier Class 5s have an express at Bromsgrove station on 5th September 1959. The leading engine is no. 45105. Photograph by Geoff Warnes.

Above BROMFORD BRIDGE STATION

In 1962, BR Standard Class 9F no. 92206 is tested by the rising gradient at Bromford Bridge and has assistance at the rear of this tanker train. Photograph courtesy Rail Photoprints.

Below BROMSGROVE STATION

A reserve of steam has developed whilst BR Standard Class 9F no. 92082 has descended Lickey Incline with this freight service and reached Bromsgrove station on 2nd March 1963. Photograph by Richard Postill.

Above BROMSGROVE STATION
A train of coal wagons has reached Bromsgrove station behind Fowler 4F 0-6-0 no. 44211 on 2nd March 1963. Photograph by Richard Postill.

Below BROMSGROVE STATION
Saltley-allocated Fowler 4F no. 44580 has a freight service at Bromsgrove station on 2nd March 1963. Photograph by Richard Postill.

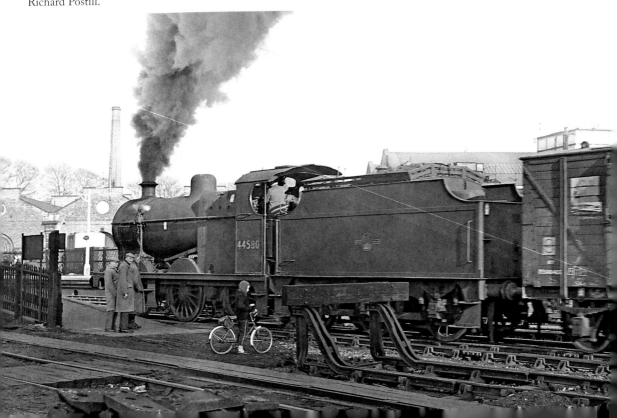

Above BROMSGROVE STATION

A pair of resident 9400 Class 0-6-0PT engines are at the rear of a train just ascending the Lickey incline from Bromsgrove station in early September 1962. Photograph by Geoff Warnes.

Below BROMSGROVE STATION

The southbound 'Devonian' rushes through Bromsgrove station behind Stanier Class 5 no. 44983 on 7th June 1960. The locomotive would hand over this Bradford-Paignton service to the Western Region at Bristol. Photograph by Ian Turnbull courtesy Rail Photoprints.

Above BURTON-ON-TRENT
On 20th September 1965, Stanier 8F no. 48507 has a train of bolster wagons loaded with steel at Burton-on-Trent. Photograph by Bill Wright.

Below BURTON-ON-TRENT
Westhouses-allocated Stanier 8F no. 48196 is serviced at Burton-on-Trent shed on 1st April 1965. The engine was withdrawn at the depot during October 1966. Photograph by Bill Wright.

Above BURTON-ON-TRENT SHED

Work-worn Stanier 8F no. 48339 is in the shed yard at Burton-on-Trent shed on 1st April 1965. A BR Type 2 (Class 25) diesel electric, D7584, is lurking in the background. Photograph by Bill Wright.

Below BURTON-ON-TRENT SHED

Minus the second pair of coupled wheels at Burton-on-Trent shed on 1st April 1965 is BR Standard Class 9F no. 92043. Allocated to Annesley at this time, the locomotive had a brief residency at Burton in early 1966 before a final six-month stay at Carlisle Kingmoor. Photograph by Bill Wright.

Above and Below BURTON-ON-TRENT, BASS BREWERY

Two well-presented locomotives are at work amidst the Bass Brewery site, Burton-on-Trent. The company's first locomotive was bought in 1863 and the number grew through to the end of the century. No. 7 (above) was bought new in 1875 as an 0-4-0WT and later rebuilt. No. 2 (below) was in service by 1900 and survived until 1964; no. 7 was scrapped in 1963. Both photographs by Bill Reed.

Above and Below BURTON-ON-TRENT STATION
The first station opened at Burton-on-Trent belonged to the Birmingham & Derby Junction Railway and was operational from 1839. This did not meet the requirements of the successor Midland Railway by the early 1880s and the company rebuilt the station. Ivatt Class 2MT 2-6-2T no. 41328 is at Burton-on-Trent station with a push-and-pull service to Tutbury around 1959/1960. Both photographs by Bill Reed.

Above BUSHBURY

BR Standard Class 7 'Britannia' Pacific no. 70021 *Morning Star* is taking on water at Bushbury in July 1964. Afterwards, the engine transported this train to London. No. 70021 was allocated to Willesden at the time, though the next move to Crewe was six months away. The engine was transferred progressively northward to reach Carlisle in June 1967, only to be condemned at the end of the year. Photograph by Brian Robbins courtesy Rail Photoprints.

Opposite above and Below CHATTERLEY

In 1864, the North Staffordshire Railway added Tunstall station to the main line between Stoke-on-Trent and Macclesfield for passengers to the nearby town. Not ten years later, the company built a new loop line, which featured a station to better serve Tunstall, and the original stop was renamed Chatterley. Being inconveniently sited undoubtedly led to an early closure in September 1948. The two images on page 41 have been taken at the station remains, with BR Standard Class 4 no. 75035 above with a northbound coal train on 16th May 1966. Below, Stanier Class 5 no. 44680 has a down freight. The area was quite industrialised, with Goldendale Iron Works just south east of the station site, as well as several collieries and brickworks south west; these were accessed by rail from Chatterley Junction. Both photographs by Bill Wright.

Above COVENTRY STATION

Just over a year had elapsed from the opening of the revamped Coventry station when this image of rebuilt 'Patriot' Class 4-6-0 no. 45545 *Planet* was taken on 23rd October 1963. The original station from 1840, which had survived the devastating air raid on the city during the war, was demolished for the modern building and platforms to be built to the design of W.R. Headley, who was also responsible for similar projects carried out at this time, such as the rebuilding of Euston. Photograph by Neville Simms from the Ranwell Collection courtesy Rail Photoprints.

Opposite above CHATTERLEY

Due to problems with Harecastle tunnel, a short distance north of the Chatterley station site, a diversion was built in the mid-1960s just to the west of the original line, running around a mile long. The switchover was not far away on 16th May 1966, with the original section closing in late June. Ivatt Class 4 2-6-0 no. 43115 has a southbound freight at Chatterley. Photograph by Bill Wright.

Opposite below CODSALL STATION

A Paddington to Birkenhead express passes through Codsall station in July 1966. Stanier Class 5 no. 45004 is just going under the station footbridge which was installed by the Great Western Railway in the early 1880s and subsequently listed, along with the station; the latter has since become a pub. Photograph by Brian Robbins courtesy Rail Photoprints.

Above CODSALL

BR Standard Class 5 4-6-0 no. 73025 is at Codsall with a Shrewsbury to Oxley freight in July 1965. Photograph by Brian Robbins courtesy Rail Photoprints.

Below COVENTRY STATION

A special from Barrow-in-Furness is ready to return northward from Coventry station on 7th May 1965. The locomotive is BR Standard Class 6 'Clan' Pacific no. 72005 *Clan MacGregor*. Photograph by Neville Simms from the Ranwell Collection courtesy Rail Photoprints.

Above COVENTRY STATION

Another special has brought Gresley V2 Class 2-6-2 no. 60810 to Coventry station on 22nd April 1963. The attraction was principally the recently consecrated cathedral. Photograph by Neville Simms from the Ranwell Collection courtesy Rail Photoprints.

Below DUDLEY STATION

An autotrain service from Dudley Port station is at Dudley station on 24th March 1951. Ivatt Class 2MT 2-6-2T no. 41226, which has the small 'British Railways' lettering, is the motive power. Photograph by B.W.L. Brooksbank.

DUDLEY STATION

Stanier 'Jubilee' Class 4-6-0 no. 45598 *Basutoland* has a special for Dudley Zoo at Dudley station during the early 1960s. Photograph by Bill Reed.

Above EVESHAM STATION
An express headed by Collett 'Castle' Class 4-6-0 no. 5057 *Earl Waldegrave* is at Evesham station on 1st June 1960. Photograph courtesy Colour-Rail.

Below ELSON
Collett 1400 Class 0-4-2T no. 1438 approaches Elson Halt on the Wrexham-Ellesmere line on 19th April 1960. Photograph by A.J.B. Dodd courtesy Rail Photoprints.

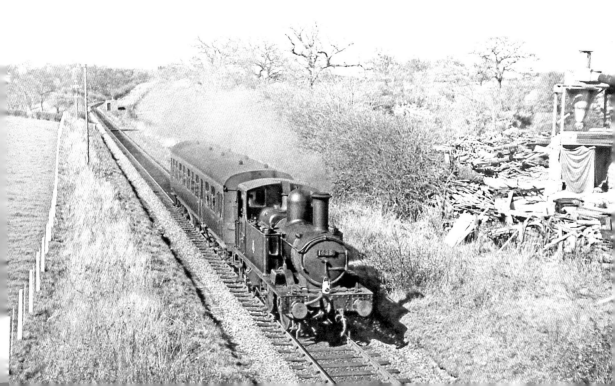

Above EARDISLEY STATION

The tablet is exchanged at Eardisley station on 6th June 1960. Ivatt Class 2 2-6-0 no. 46506 is with the 10.25 service from Brecon to Hereford. Photograph by Hugh Ballantyne courtesy Rail Photoprints.

Below FENNY COMPTON

An iron ore train bound for South Wales nears Fenny Compton behind Collett 2884 Class 2-8-0 no. 2897 during 1958. Photograph from the Dave Cobbe Collection courtesy Rail Photoprints.

Above GRANVILLE COLLIERY

Two Hunslet 0-6-0ST locomotives are at the Granville Colliery shed in August 1967. No. 3 (works no. 3789, built 1953) is outside the building, whilst no. 16 (no. 2895, built 1943) stands on the right. Photograph by A.J.B. Dodd courtesy Rail Photoprints.

Below HANDSWORTH

Churchward 4300 Class 2-6-0 no. 6364 has a train at Handsworth (near Queens Head Road) on 29th June 1964. Photograph by Richard Postill.

HATTON BANK

For several miles west of Warwick the line rose at gradients around 1 in 100 to reach a summit at Hatton. Collett 'Castle' Class no. 5056 *Earl Baldwin* is tackling this section on 28th April 1963. Photograph by Neville Simms from the Ranwell Collection courtesy Rail Photoprints.

Above HANDSWORTH

Worcester-based 'Castle' no. 5054 *Earl of Ducie* has an express at Handsworth on 17th July 1964. The engine had a month at Gloucester shed before withdrawn in October. Photograph by Richard Postill.

Below HANDSWORTH

View south east from Handsworth Queens Head signal box, with the loop from the Birmingham-Wolverhampton line to the original Grand Junction Railway route in the background, on 23rd July 1964. The box controlled the main lines in the area, as well as the nearby Queens Head sidings. BR 9F no. 92137 has a westbound Class K train. Photograph by Richard Postill.

Above HENLEY-IN-ARDEN

When Charles Collett retired as CME of the Great Western Railway in 1941, F.W. Hawksworth, who had been with the company all his life, was promoted to the position. His first design – the 6959 Class or 'Modified Hall' – was an improved version of his predecessor's 'Hall' Class 4-6-0. Several changes were made to bring the design towards modern practices, such as new chassis, altered bogie and larger superheater. The first appeared from Swindon Works in early 1944. Whilst a dozen were completed during the year, the number did not grow significantly until 1947 when a steady stream of engines entered traffic; a total of 71 were ultimately at work across the system. No. 7918 *Rhose Wood Hall* features here and has an express at Henley-in-Arden on 6th April 1957. The locomotive was erected in April 1950 and was dispatched to Tyseley to begin service. No. 7918 remained employed there until withdrawn in February 1965. Photograph courtesy Rail Photoprints.

Opposite above HEREFORD STATION

A local service is at Hereford station in July 1963. Coupled to the train is Collett 2251 Class 0-6-0 no. 2286, whose driver appears to be under interrogation from a group of young enthusiasts. The engine had been at Hereford shed for almost a year at this point and was condemned there in September 1964. Photograph courtesy Colour-Rail.

Opposite below HEREFORD SHED

Several locomotives are out of service at Hereford shed on 21st August 1963. Closest is Collett 7400 Class 0-6-0PT no. 7446, followed by classmate no. 7437, Collett 8750 Class 0-6-0PT no. 9665 and no. 9717. Next is Churchward 'Star' – rebuilt as a 'Castle' – no. 5092 *Tresco Abbey* and finally Collett 1400 0-4-2T no. 1458. Both the 8750 Class engines were withdrawn at this time, along with no. 5092, whilst no. 7446 and 1458 would be at work until July and November 1964 respectively. No. 7437 survived until March 1965. Photograph courtesy Colour-Rail.

HOLLINSWOOD

East of Telford at Hollinswood, BR Standard Class 4 no. 75053 has a Shrewsbury–Birmingham express in July 1965. Photograph by A.J.B. Dodd courtesy Rail Photoprints.

Above HONEYBOURNE

For around five miles between Honeybourne and Campden on the Oxford-Worcester line, a gradient of 1 in 100 was encountered by trains travelling to Oxford. 2251 Class 0-6-0 no. 2244 is providing assistance to a freight train on 7th November 1964. Photograph by Richard Postill.

Below HILLMORTON

'Jubilee' Class no. 45554 *Ontario* approaches Rugby through the eastern suburb of Hillmorton on 17th August 1963. Photograph by Neville Simms from the Ranwell Collection courtesy Rail Photoprints.

Above **KING'S NORTON**
Travelling northward towards King's Norton on 21st December 1963 is Fowler 4F Class 0-6-0 no. 44428. The locomotive was erected at Derby Works in October 1927 and was in service until February 1964. Allocated to Derby shed for most of the 1950s, no. 44428 made a final transfer to Rowsley in July 1960 and was later withdrawn there. Photograph by Richard Postill.

Opposite above **KIDDERMINSTER STATION**
View northward at Kidderminster station on 12th June 1962. Collett 8750 Class 0-6-0PT no. 3607 is in a servicing area on the eastern side of the line, with Yew Tree Road in the background. The station was opened by the Oxford, Worcester & Wolverhampton Railway in mid-1852 and the building was rebuilt at the end of the decade, only to fall victim to a fire. The new station then served passengers for over 100 years until replaced by BR. Kidderminster station is now adjacent to Kidderminster Town which serves the heritage Severn Valley Railway. No. 3607 was Kidderminster-allocated when pictured and in service until October 1966, being condemned at Tyseley. Photograph by Bill Reed.

Opposite below **KIDDERMINSTER**
Collett 2884 Class 2-8-0 no. 2891 has a northbound freight train at Kidderminster on 12th June 1962. The locomotive is passing the imposing goods depot just south of Kidderminster station. In the mid-1980s, the building was taken over by the Severn Valley Railway and used as a place to restore carriages. No. 2891, a long time Cardiff resident, was withdrawn from Cardiff East Dock in October 1964. Photograph by Bill Reed.

Above LAWLEY BANK STATION

A small branch connected the Worcester-Shrewsbury line at Buildwas and the Wolverhampton-Shrewsbury line near Wellington. Several small stations were on the branch, which was built by the Wellington & Severn Junction Railway, including Lawley Bank station. Collett 8750 Class no. 9639 has a service for Wellington there and is waiting for a signal releasing the train during 1961. The signalman has likely held the train a bit longer to procure some coal and he has the scuttle ready for the fireman here. Photograph by A.J.B. Dodd courtesy Rail Photoprints.

Opposite above LAPWORTH

As train weights increased at the turn of the century, the permanent way departments on several lines were unable to keep pace with providing structures able to withstand greater forces acting on them. The GWR was no different and Churchward was prevented from building a suitable express passenger locomotive to meet the running department's needs during the First World War. When improvements were finally made to a number of bridges on the GWR system, Collett introduced the 'King' Class 4-6-0 in 1927. These were very powerful locomotives compared to their contemporaries and possessed a 6ft diameter boiler, with a working pressure of 250 lb per sq. in., feeding four 16¼ in. by 28 in. cylinders, along with 6 ft 6 in. diameter driving wheels, which resulted in a tractive effort of just over 40,000 lbf, though this was later slightly reduced. An unidentified class member has a southbound express near Lapworth on 14th April 1962. Photograph by Richard Postill.

Opposite below LEAMINGTON SPA STATION

Collett 'Hall' Class no. 6917 *Oldlands Hall* is at Leamington Spa station on 5th October 1963. The locomotive still had nearly three years left in service and was condemned at Banbury shed; no. 6917 was based at Oxley when pictured here. Photograph by Richard Postill.

LEAMINGTON SPA STATION

The 'Cambrian Coast Express' is at Leamington Spa station, c. 1960, with Collett 'King' Class no. 6029 *King Edward VIII*. Photograph by Bill Reed.

Above LEAMINGTON SPA STATION
Built at Swindon in July 1937, 'Castle' Class no. 5067 *St Fagans Castle* was in service until July 1962. For the final year in service, the engine was based at Reading shed and has the depot's '81D' code attached to the smokebox door here at Leamington Spa station. Photograph by Bill Reed.

Below LEAMINGTON SPA STATION
'King' Class no. 6011 *King James I* has an express at Leamington Spa station. Photograph by Bill Reed.

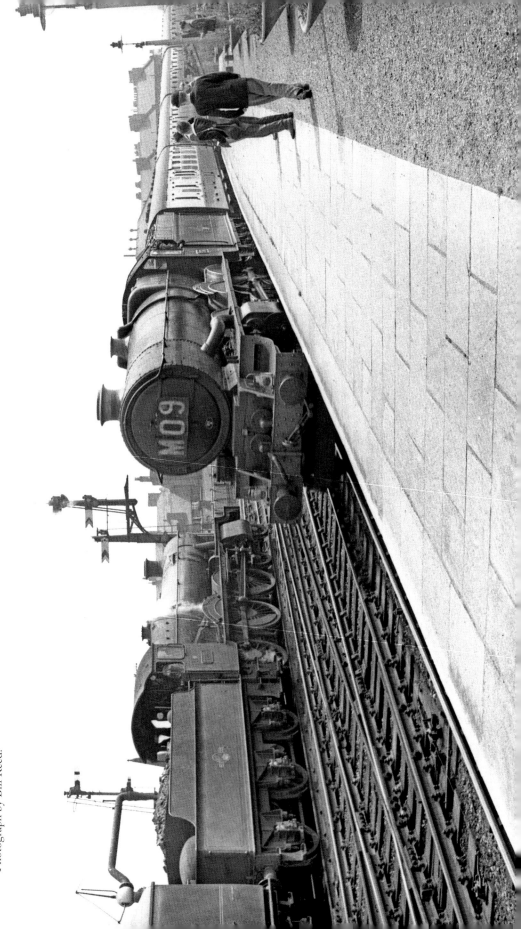

LEAMINGTON SPA STATION
'King' Class no. 6023 *King Edward II* pulls into Leamington Spa station with an express on 5th September 1961. Photograph by Bill Reed.

Above LEATON

The long-closed station at Leaton is passed by Stanier Class 5 no. 44838 on 30th August 1966. The locomotive has the 14.25 Birkenhead to Paddington express. Photograph by Hugh Ballantyne courtesy Rail Photoprints.

Below LEEBOTWOOD

Stanier 4P Class 2-6-4T no. 42390 has a Shrewsbury-Swansea service at Leebotwood in April 1958. Photograph by A.E. Durrant courtesy Rail Photoprints.

Above LEEK BROOK JUNCTION

The West Midlands Branch of the Railway Correspondence & Travel Society elected for the comfort of several brake vans for a tour of the Stoke-on-Trent area on 29th October 1966. Here, Ivatt Class 2MT no. 41204 has the train at Leek Brook Junction (north east of Stoke). Photograph courtesy Colour-Rail.

Below LEOMINSTER

Although closed from 1952, the line between Bromyard and Leominster remained intact until 1958 when lifted. Before this occurred, the Stephenson Locomotive Society organised a special for 26th April. The locomotive chosen was 4500 Class 2-6-2T no. 4571, which is turned at Leominster here. Photograph courtesy Colour-Rail.

Above LEDBURY

Collett 5205 Class 2-8-0T no. 5243 is at Ledbury shed on 8th November 1958. The engine was used to bank trains through Ledbury Tunnel. Photograph by B.W.L. Brooksbank.

Below LEDBURY STATION

A service bound for Hereford makes a stop at Ledbury station on 11th July 1959. 'Castle' Class no. 7005 *Sir Edward Elgar* is hauling the train. Photograph by Hugh Ballantyne courtesy Rail Photoprints.

Above LICHFIELD TRENT VALLEY STATION

Stanier 8F Class no. 48171 has an express freight at Lichfield Trent Valley station in June 1962. The locomotive is passing under the electrification gantries then being installed as part of the West Coast Electrification Scheme. The first section to open was between Crewe and Manchester in 1960, then being extended to Liverpool in 1962 and London by 1965. The project was not fully completed until 1974 as the line north of Liverpool to Glasgow was electrified. Photograph by Richard Postill.

Opposite LICHFIELD TRENT VALLEY STATION

The London, Midland & Scottish Railway lagged behind the competitor companies' outlook on express passenger locomotives after Grouping in 1923. Most had competent 4-6-0s and even Pacifics to work the trains, yet the LMSR relied on 4-4-0s and inadequate 'Claughton' Class 4-6-0s. In the mid-1920s, the North British Locomotive Company was tasked with producing a suitable express locomotive and the first of these appeared in 1927, with a total of 50 erected in Glasgow during the latter part of the year; Derby Works later added 20 engines to the class total. The 'Royal Scot' Class subsequently proved capable and were on the principal expresses for around ten years until replaced by Stanier 'Coronation' Class Pacifics. To give the 'Royal Scots' a new lease of life in the mid-1940s, several were rebuilt with a standard boiler and cylinders. This proved successful and was class-wide, being completed in the mid-1950s. No. 46115 *Scots Guardsman* was sent into traffic during October 1927 and was rebuilt nearly 20 years later. The engine is at Lichfield Trent Valley station in June 1962 and was allocated to Longsight depot, Manchester, at the time. When withdrawn in January 1966, the engine was purchased for preservation and has been particularly active in recent years. Photograph by Richard Postill.

Above LICKEY INCLINE
Fowler 4F Class 0-6-0 no. 44245 coasts down the Lickey incline with a local service on 5th September 1959. Photograph by Geoff Warnes.

Opposite LICKEY INCLINE
Two 9400 Class 0-6-0PT locomotives assist a train up the Lickey incline on 8th September 1962. Photograph by Geoff Warnes.

LICKEY INCLINE
BR Standard Class 9F no. 92231 pushes the rear of this passenger train up Lickey incline on 5th September 1959. Photograph by Geoff Warnes.

Above LICKEY INCLINE

Two bankers drop back down Lickey incline after assisting a train on 29th August 1959. The engines are Collett 5205 Class no. 5226 and Fowler 3F no. 47308. Photograph by Geoff Warnes.

Below LICKEY INCLINE

Hughes 'Crab' Class 2-6-0 no. 42900 drags a train of empty coal wagons up Lickey bank with the assistance of BR 9F no. 92079 on 8th September 1962. Photograph by Geoff Warnes.

LICKEY INCLINE
Around a third of the way up Lickey incline, 'Stanier Jubilee' Class no. 45564 *New South Wales* forges ahead with an express on 8th September 1962. Photograph by Geoff Warnes.

Above LICKEY INCLINE
A quartet of Hawksworth 9400 Class 0-6-0PT engines travel back to the bottom of Lickey incline on 8th September 1962. They are: no. 9443, no. 8402, no. 8403 and no. 8405. Photograph by Geoff Warnes.

Below LICKEY INCLINE
Several passengers keep a keen eye on the progress of their passenger train up Lickey bank on 5th September 1959 as BR 9F no. 92231 provides a helping hand. Photograph by Geoff Warnes.

LITTLETON COLLIERY

Manning Wardle 0-6-0ST locomotive *Littleton No. 5* was new to Littleton Colliery in 1922 and still at work when this image was captured in June 1971. Photograph by Bill Reed.

Above LITTLETON COLLIERY
Robert Nelson No. 4 shunts wagons at Littleton Colliery in June 1971. The locomotive was transferred to the colliery in early 1959. Photograph by Bill Reed.

Below LITTLETON COLLIERY
North west of Cannock, Littleton Colliery was sunk near the village of Huntington in 1877 and operations continued to the early 1990s. Hudswell Clarke 0-6-0ST no. 7 is at work there in June 1971. Photograph by Bill Reed.

Above MADELEY (STAFFORDSHIRE)

View north from the lineside near Manor Road, Madeley, as two Stanier 8F Class 2-8-0s pass by with a freight train on 20th May 1961. Leading is no. 48074 and behind is no. 48398, both engines being allocated to Nuneaton shed at this time. Madeley was located a short distance south of Crewe on the West Coast Main Line and a station originally served the village, though this closed in 1952. Photograph by Hugh Ballantyne courtesy Rail Photoprints.

Opposite MADELEY JUNCTION (SHROPSHIRE)

Collett 'Manor' Class 4-6-0 no. 7821 *Ditcheat Manor* comes off the Madeley branch at Madeley Junction in July 1965. The line left the GWR Wolverhampton-Shrewsbury route west of Shifnal – now east of Telford – and ran southward to meet the Buildwas-Wellington branch at Lightmoor Junction. Several collieries were mainly served by the route, although at one time passenger trains operated, but these had disappeared by Grouping. No. 7821, which has a short train of coal wagons bound for Wolverhampton, had less than six months left in service and has already lost the nameplate. Photograph by A.J.B. Dodd courtesy Rail Photoprints.

Above MOORHAMPTON STATION

The Hereford, Hay & Brecon Railway was promoted in the late 1850s and received an Act to build the line in 1859, with a projected cost of nearly £300,000 for the 34 miles of track. The first section between Hereford and Moorhampton was ready for traffic in late October 1862, followed by Eardisley in June 1863 and Hay a year later. Soon afterwards, an extension was made to reach the Mid-Wales Railway at Three Cocks Junction and from there to Brecon. Ivatt Class 2MT 2-6-0 no. 46506 has a train that has picked up passengers changing at Three Cocks Junction for Hereford on 6th June 1960 and is making a stop at Moorhampton station. The locomotive had entered service from Swindon Works in November 1952 and allocated to Oswestry. After several moves, mainly in the North West during the 1960s, no. 46506 was condemned at Newton Heath shed in May 1967. Photograph by Hugh Ballantyne courtesy Rail Photoprints.

Above MUCH WENLOCK STATION

On the line between Buildwas and Craven Arms, Much Wenlock station was opened in 1866. A local service for Wellington is at the station during April 1960, with Collett 5700 Class 0-6-0PT no. 5764 at the head of the train. The locomotive was soon to be withdrawn and was bought by London Transport. At work for another ten years as L95, the engine was subsequently preserved at the Severn Valley Railway. Photograph by A.J.B. Dodd courtesy Rail Photoprints.

Above NEWPORT STATION (SHROPSHIRE)

An odd pairing arrives at Newport station on 20th December 1960. Rebuilt 'Royal Scot' no. 46114 *Coldstream Guardsman* is with the 11.25 local train from Shrewsbury to Stafford. The locomotive was allocated to Liverpool Edge Hill at the time, making the appearance here anomalous. Newport station opened in 1849 on the London & North Western Railway-operated line from Stafford to Shrewsbury via Wellington. The facility served the market town until 1964, whilst the route was later closed and the track lifted. No. 46114 survived until September 1963. Photograph by Hugh Ballantyne courtesy Rail Photoprints.

Opposite above NUNEATON TRENT VALLEY STATION

A southbound local service arrives at Nuneaton Trent Valley station on 28th April 1951. The locomotive is Nuneaton-allocated Ivatt Class 2MT 2-6-2T no. 41236. Built at Crewe Works in September 1949, the engine was to move on to Llandudno Junction in August 1952 and for the most part remained there until condemned in November 1962. Photograph by B.W.L. Brooksbank.

Opposite below NUNEATON TRENT VALLEY STATION

Stanier Class 5 no. 45282 is at the north end of Nuneaton Trent Valley station with a workman's train on 28th April 1951. Although open from 1847, Nuneaton station was rebuilt in 1874 and 1915 to cope with increased traffic, whilst the 'Trent Valley' portion of the title was in use between 1924 and 1969. This was due to the LMSR absorbing the Midland Railway's Nuneaton Midland station, which became Nuneaton Abbey Street until closure in the late 1960s. Photograph by B.W.L. Brooksbank.

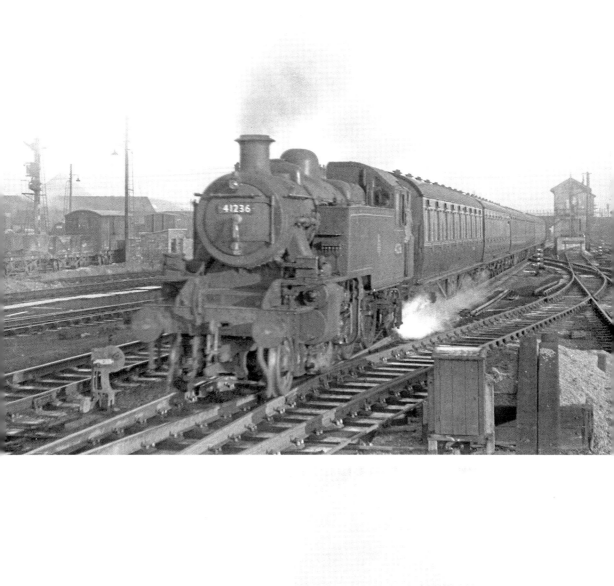

Above NUNEATON TRENT VALLEY STATION

The locomotive Club of Great Britain organised the 'Severn and Dee' railtour for 26th February 1967. Travelling from London to Nuneaton behind an electric locomotive, Stanier Class 5 no. 44944 took the train on to Wolverhampton where recently preserved 'Castle' no. 7029 *Clun Castle* was waiting. BR Standard Class 9F no. 92026 met the party at Chester and transported the group to Crewe where the day with steam ended. No. 44944 was Oxley-allocated at the time, though soon moved on to Chester, followed quickly by a transfer to Crewe, where the engine was withdrawn in September. Photograph by Tony Martens courtesy John Law.

Opposite above NUNEATON TRENT VALLEY STATION

Rebuilt 'Royal Scot' no. 46132 *The King's Regiment, Liverpool* approaches Nuneaton Trent Valley station with the 07.50 Crewe to Euston passenger service on 28th April 1951. The locomotive was amongst the first batch of rebuilds in 1943, with the transformation taking place late in the year, and no. 46132 ran without smoke deflectors until October 1951. In the background on the right is Nuneaton No. 3 signal box, whilst on the extreme right the banking carrying the ex-Midland Railway line between Birmingham and Leicester over the WCML to Nuneaton Abbey Street station is visible. Photograph by B.W.L. Brooksbank.

Opposite below NUNEATON TRENT VALLEY STATION

Although completed at Crewe Works in July 1954, BR Standard Class Pacific no. 70048 had to wait four years before receiving a name, being amongst the few class members not to be christened when new. On 22nd July 1958, the Duke of Norfolk conducted a ceremony at Euston bestowing the name *The Territorial Army 1908-1958* on the engine. No. 70048 is pictured here at Nuneaton Trent Valley station with an express on 13th August 1964. Photograph by Cedric Clayson courtesy John Clayson.

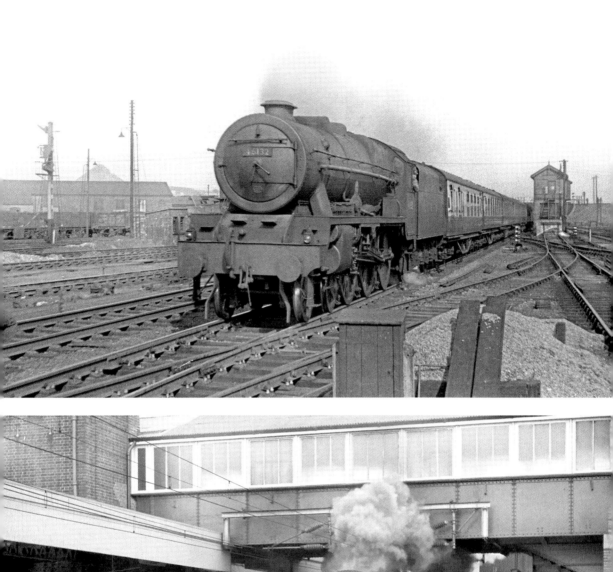

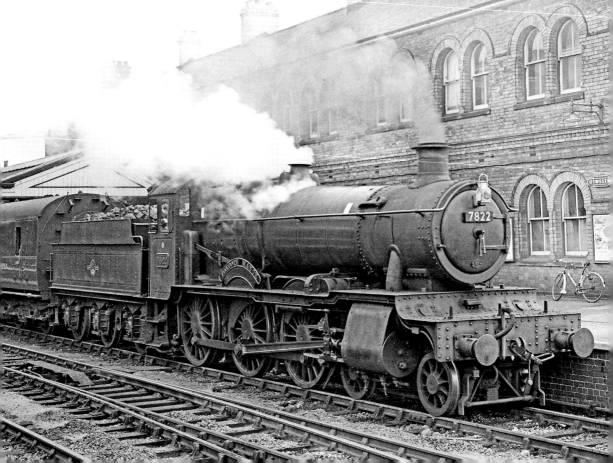

Above OSWESTRY STATION

Collett 1400 Class 0-4-2T no. 1458 departs from Oswestry station with a local service on 29th September 1962, whilst Collett 9300 Class 2-6-0 no. 7329 waits to leave with another local train. The latter had been rebuilt in 1956 to increase the route availability, as were all the 9300 Class engines in the late 1950s. Photograph from the Dave Cobbe Collection courtesy Rail Photoprints.

Opposite above NUNEATON TRENT VALLEY STATION

An early evening express is at Nuneaton Trent Valley station on 26th March 1964. The locomotive, whose crew is saluted by a 'spotter' on the platform, is BR Standard Class 7 'Britannia' Pacific no. 70050 *Firth of Clyde*. Amongst the last class members sent into traffic during mid-summer 1954, the engine was nearly ten years at work in Scotland at Glasgow Polmadie shed and later transferred to England, with spells at Holyhead, Crewe, Banbury and Carlisle before withdrawn in August 1966. Photograph by Cedric Clayson courtesy John Clayson.

Opposite below OSWESTRY STATION

Introduced just before the Second World War, Collett's 7800 'Manor' Class was a lightweight 4-6-0 intended for mixed traffic duties across the system, possessing a greater route availability than other classes with the wheel arrangement. There was an initial batch of 20 built at Swindon, followed by another ten after Nationalisation. No. 7822 *Foxcote Manor* was amongst the latter batch, entering service to Oswestry in December 1950. During 1954, the engine moved on to Chester, but later returned to Oswestry and was still employed there when pictured at the town's station in 1960 with a local service. After a year at Machynlleth, no. 7822 transferred to Shrewsbury and was condemned there at the end of 1965. Photograph courtesy Rail Photoprints.

Above OSWESTRY STATION

Enthusiasts race to obtain a picture of Collett 'Manor' Class no. 7802 *Bradley Manor* on 17th January 1965. The locomotive is at Oswestry station with the Stephenson Locomotive Society's 'Farewell to the Cambrian Railways' railtour. No. 7802 was the main engine employed and transported the passengers from Shrewsbury to Welshpool, then northward to Oswestry, meeting the Cambrian Railway's branch for Ellesmere and Whitchurch, which subsequently closed. Returning from the latter place to Oswestry, Ivatt Class 2MT no. 46512 was coupled to the train for a short run on the also redundant Llanfyllin branch. No. 7802 survived in service until November 1965 when dispatched to Barry for scrapping. The engine was later rescued from there and returned to steam, serving the Severn Valley Railway for much of the last 30 years. Photograph by Richard Postill.

Opposite OSWESTRY

A number of locomotives stored in sidings at Oswestry have been caught from a passing train on 22nd June 1964. The two closest are Collett 5101 Class 2-6-2T no. 4148 and 'Hall' Class no. 6930 *Aldersley Hall*, which had been involved in a collision and awaiting attention from the former Cambrian Railways workshops at Oswestry. In the background on the left is Collett 7400 Class 0-6-0PT no. 7428, with the locomotive decorated in GWR livery specially for working as the station pilot at Aberystwyth. No. 7428 had been withdrawn over 18 months earlier and is still to be scrapped, whilst no. 4148 and 6930 returned to traffic to be condemned in September and October 1965 respectively. Photograph by David Christie.

Opposite above OSWESTRY STATION

The Shrewsbury & Chester Railway was the first to reach Oswestry in 1849. This was followed by the Oswestry & Newtown Railway which opened the first section of line from the town to Pool Clay in 1860 and later completed in 1864. The railway was later a constituent of the Cambrian Railways and the company based itself at Oswestry station. Collett 1400 Class no. 1432 has a local service at Oswestry on 3rd October 1955. Photograph by Bill Reed.

Opposite below OSWESTRY STATION

Oswestry station closed to passengers in 1966 and freight five years later. Following a period in private use, the station returned to railway operations in 2014 with the establishment of Cambrian Heritage Railways. On 3rd October 1955, 'Dean Goods' 0-6-0 no. 2538 has a ballast train at the station. Photograph by Bill Reed.

Below OSWESTRY STATION

Whilst the photographer was waiting for his Shrewsbury to Crewe train to leave Oswestry, Ivatt Class 2MT no. 46514 was pictured arriving at the station with a local service on 22nd June 1964. The locomotive was based at Oswestry shed when new in December 1952 and was employed there until January 1965 when transferred to Newton Heath. Further moves to Lancaster and Carnforth occurred before withdrawal in June 1966. Photograph by David Christie.

OXLEY SHED

BR Standard Class 5 4-6-0 no. 73019 is stored inside Oxley shed during May 1966. The engine returned to service during the month and saw out the year before condemned at Bolton. Photograph by Brian Robbins courtesy Rail Photoprints.

Above OXLEY SIDINGS
Ivatt Class 4MT no. 43115 is at Oxley sidings with a freight train bound for Birmingham on 27th November 1965. Photograph by Brian Robbins courtesy Rail Photoprints.

Below OXLEY SHED
Located a distance to the north west of Wolverhampton, Oxley shed was built by the Great Western Railway, opening in 1907 and was a large building that housed two turntables with radiating roads. Being close to Oxley sidings, a large number of GWR freight types were accommodated and latterly some ex-LMSR freight engines. Several 0-6-0PTs are in the shed during April 1965, along with a Stanier Class 5. Photograph courtesy Rail Photoprints.

OXLEY SIDINGS

A Class H freight train is pulled out of Oxley sidings by 'Hall' Class no. 6906 *Chicheley Hall* on 22nd June 1963. Photograph by Richard Postill.

Above OXLEY SHED

Two lines of withdrawn locomotives are pictured at Oxley shed on 26th March 1967, which was the month of closure for the depot. From left to right the group includes: no. 48177, no. 45283, no. 44808, no. 44919 and no. 44856. Photograph by David Rostance courtesy Rail Photoprints.

Below PERSHORE STATION

At Pershore station (east of Worcester), 'Modified Hall' no. 6960 *Raveningham Hall* makes a stop with the 13.25 local between Oxford and Worcester on 25th April 1964. Photograph by Ian Turnbull courtesy Rail Photoprints.

Above POLESWORTH

Stanier 'Jubilee' Class no. 45702 *Colossus* has an express at Polesworth (east of Tamworth) on 3rd June 1955. Photograph by Bill Reed.

Below POLESWORTH

The 10.00 departure from Euston was traditionally the express to Glasgow, with a corresponding train running from Scotland. Whilst the similar service on the East Coast Main Line was known as the 'Flying Scotsman' for many years, the West Coast train was not named until 1927 as the 'Royal Scot'. The train is at Polesworth on 3rd June 1955 behind Stanier 'Coronation' Class Pacific no. 46237 *City of Bristol*. Photograph by Bill Reed.

Above ROSS-ON-WYE STATION
The 10.25 Hereford-Gloucester train arrives at Ross-on-Wye station on 3rd January 1959. Collett 5101 Class no. 5177 of Gloucester shed is leading. Photograph by Hugh Ballantyne courtesy Rail Photoprints.

Below ROSS-ON-WYE STATION
On 26th March 1964 Collett 5101 Class no. 4161 stands at Ross-on-Wye station with the 16.00 Gloucester-Hereford service. The station was closed before the end of the year, whilst the line from Monmouth (removed from the station sign – see above) had trains withdrawn five years earlier. Photograph by Hugh Ballantyne courtesy Rail Photoprints.

RUGBY CLIFTON ROAD

East of Rugby station at Clifton Road, Stanier 'Coronation' Pacific no. 46244 *George VI* passes by with an express. Photograph by Bill Reed.

Above RUGBY SHED

Work-worn Johnson 2F (MR 1357 Class) 0-6-0 no. 58215 is between duties at Rugby shed around mid-1960. The engine was a recent arrival at the depot, though withdrawal occurred in March 1961. Photograph by Bill Reed.

Below RUGBY SHED

Stanier 3P Class 2-6-2T no. 40207 is at Rugby shed c. 1960. Built at Crewe Works in April 1938, the locomotive was in service until February 1962. Photograph by Bill Reed.

RUGBY CLIFTON ROAD
A southbound express gathers speed away from Rugby behind Stanier 'Jubilee' no. 45631 *Tanganyika*. Photograph by Bill Reed.

Above RUGBY

A northbound local service departs from Rugby on 9th September 1961 with Stanier 4P Class 2-6-4T no. 42562. Photograph by Neville Simms from the Ranwell Collection courtesy Rail Photoprints.

Below RUGBY SHED

Fowler 'Patriot' Class no. 45541 *Duke of Sutherland* is between duties at Rugby shed around mid-1960. Photograph by Bill Reed.

RUGBY CLIFTON ROAD
'Coronation' Class Pacific no. 46245 *City of London* has the 'Royal Scot' express east of Rugby c. 1960. Photograph by Bill Reed.

Above RUGBY MIDLAND STATION
Rebuilt 'Royal Scot' no. 46120 *Royal Inniskilling Fusilier* is at Rugby Midland station with a train of empty stock on 23rd December 1961. Photograph by Neville Simms from the Ranwell Collection courtesy Rail Photoprints.

Below RUGBY CENTRAL STATION
Stanier Class 5 no. 45416 moves away from Rugby Central station on 28th December 1964. Photograph by Neville Simms from the Ranwell Collection courtesy Rail Photoprints.

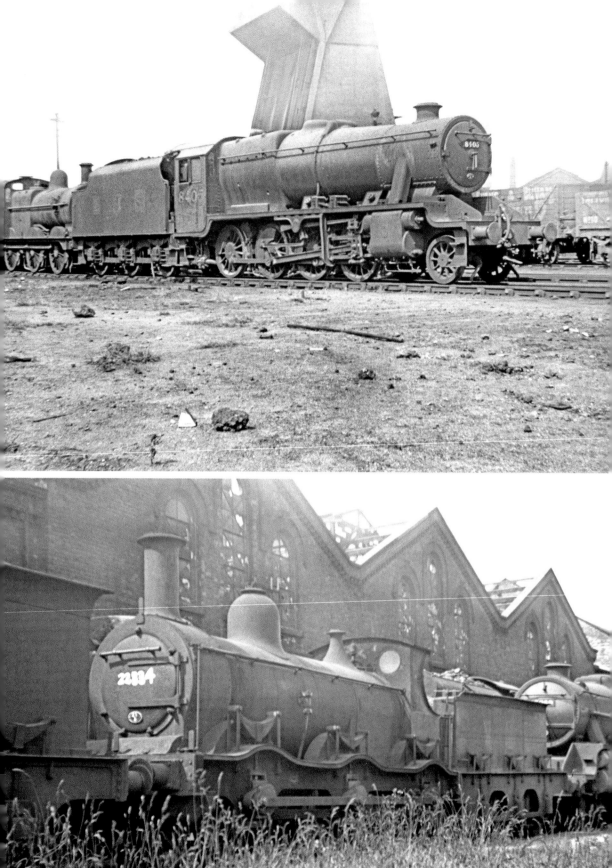

Above SALTLEY

View south from Saltley Road, near Saltley station, on 5th September 1962 as Stanier Class 5 no. 44814 approaches with a freight train. In the distance is Saltley Junction which led to Lawley Street goods station. Saltley was on the Birmingham & Derby Junction Railway line and connected with the Birmingham & Gloucester Railway. With the completion of the Midland Railway's Birmingham West Suburban Railway, the route served as a bypass from New Street station. Photograph by B.W.L. Brooksbank.

Opposite above SALTLEY SHED

To help ease the burden on the railways during the Second World War, the 'big four' companies all built Stanier 8F Class 2-8-0s and, with the exception of the Southern Railway, the class was put to work across the country. No. 8405 was erected at Swindon Works during August 1943 and employed by the GWR until December 1946 when returned to the LMSR. No. 8405 was subsequently allocated to Saltley shed and is in the yard here on 27th July 1947. The locomotive had spells at Stourton, Kirkby-in-Ashfield, Mansfield and Warrington sheds before condemned in July 1966. Photograph by B.W.L. Brooksbank.

Opposite below SALTLEY SHED

Ex-Midland Railway Kirtley 700 Class 0-6-0 no. 22834 has been abandoned at Saltley shed (pictured on 27th July 1947) and awaits withdrawal shortly before Nationalisation. The locomotive was one of 316 engines built to the design over five years, starting 1869 and no. 22834 was a later example, entering traffic in 1874. Photograph by B.W.L. Brooksbank.

Above SALTLEY SHED
Following employment on an unidentified special train, Stanier Class 5 no. 44919 is serviced at Saltley shed in November 1965. Previously, the engine had been a long-term resident at the depot, though had moved on to Oxley earlier in 1965 and was condemned there in December 1966. Photograph courtesy Rail Photoprints.

Opposite above SALTLEY SHED
The Birmingham & Derby Junction Railway was one of the constituents of the Midland Railway when the company was established in 1844. The latter built the first engine shed at Saltley, south of the station on the eastern side of the line, in the late 1860s. This was a large roundhouse and subsequently two more similar buildings were added by the turn of the century. In 1966 (a year before closure), a trio of BR Standard Class 9F 2-10-0s have gathered around one of the turntables. Photograph by Brian Robbins courtesy Rail Photoprints.

Opposite below SALTLEY
Saltley-allocated Stanier 8F no. 48220 passes Duddeston Road signal box (south of Saltley station) with a train of coal wagons in 1966. The box originally controlled a level crossing, but the installation of the engine shed and industrial developments in the area increased responsibilities. The building was of recent construction, being erected in the mid-1950s and the last of several to stand on the site. Dominating the background is Saltley Gas Works, which was closed around the late 1960s, near the same time as the signal box. Photograph by Brian Robbins courtesy Rail Photoprints.

Above SHREWSBURY STATION

Opened on 14th October 1848 by the Shrewsbury & Chester Railway, Shrewsbury station became a hub for several lines, both for the GWR and LNWR. This meant a variety of locomotives could be found at the station. Here, on 17th July 1965, Stanier Class 5 no. 45184 of Chester has worked southward with a train and is passing through Shrewsbury station. The locomotive had just three months left in service. Photograph by Richard Postill.

Opposite above SHREWSBURY STATION

Constructed at Swindon Works in September 1937, Collett 'Grange' Class no. 6838 *Goodmoor Grange* had a career spanning just over 28 years. Under BR, the locomotive worked from Plymouth until the mid-1950s when transferred between several sheds in South Wales until condemned in late 1965. No. 6838 is at Shrewsbury station here on 28th September 1963 when based at Pontypool Road depot, north of Newport. Photograph by Richard Postill.

Opposite below SHREWSBURY SHED

In spite of water accumulated in the turntable pit, BR Standard Class 4 2-6-4T no. 80097 uses the apparatus at Shrewsbury shed on 28th September 1963. Stabling facilities for locomotives had been established by the Shrewsbury & Hereford Railway in the early 1850s south of Shrewsbury station, on the east side of the line. Several extensions were built subsequently and the depot later became a joint operation under the London & North Western Railway and Great Western Railway. No. 80097 had recently transferred to Oswestry shed from Swansea and was there for a year before a final move to Machynlleth occurred. The locomotive was withdrawn in July 1965, with a service life of just over 10 years. A classmate is seen in the background on the left with the depot's breakdown crane. Photograph by Richard Postill.

SHREWSBURY STATION

'Hall' no. 6944 *Fledborough Hall* is at Shrewsbury with BR Type 4 (later Class 47) diesel no. D1586 on 22nd June 1964. Photograph by David Christie.

Above SHREWSBURY STATION

Stanier Class 5 no. 45058 acts as Shrewsbury station pilot on 12th May 1966. The engine's final year in traffic was spent at Shrewsbury, with no. 45058 condemned in October 1966. Photograph by Bill Wright.

Below SHREWSBURY STATION

'Hall' Class no. 6903 *Belmont Hall* (nameplates removed) backs on to a train at Shrewsbury station on 22nd June 1964. Photograph by David Christie.

SHREWSBURY STATION
On 12th May 1966, Stanier 8F no. 48700 passes through Shrewsbury station with the 13.45 Oxley to Croes Newydd express freight.
Photograph by Bill Wright.

Above SHREWSBURY STATION
Stanier 'Jubilee' no. 45577 *Bengal* waits patiently at the head of an express for the departure time at Shrewsbury station on 22nd June 1964. Photograph by David Christie.

Below SHREWSBURY STATION
Shrewsbury-allocated BR Standard Class 5 no. 73025 is ready to move off from the station on 22nd June 1964. Photograph by David Christie.

Above SHREWSBURY STATION

BR 9F no. 92152 is at Shrewsbury station on 22nd June 1964 with a train of oil tankers. The engine had been Saltley-allocated from new and departed for Birkenhead in late 1966. Photograph by David Christie.

Below SHREWSBURY STATION

Another view of BR Standard Class 5 no. 73025 at Shrewsbury station on 22nd June 1964. The locomotive, which has a local service, was based at Shrewsbury for much of the early 1960s and withdrawn from Patricroft in October 1967. Photograph by David Christie.

Above SOLIHULL
Stanier Class 5 no. 44805 has an express freight at Solihull. Photograph courtesy Colour-Rail.

Below SOLIHULL STATION
On 24th August 1962 – just a month away from withdrawal – 'King' Class 4-6-0 no. 6016 *King Edward V* has an express at Solihull station. Photograph courtesy Colour-Rail.

Above STAFFORD STATION
Overhead gantries are in place at Stafford station in 1962 ready for electrification, which was still some time away. Yet, a new station had been constructed and opened at Stafford during the year. Stanier 'Jubilee' no. 45669 *Fisher* is on the through line with a northbound express, passing early Type 3 diesel electric locomotive no. 10202, which was built at Ashford Works in September 1951 and soon to be condemned in December 1963. Photograph courtesy Rail Photoprints.

Opposite above SPON END
A short distance away from Coventry station at Spon End, on the Coventry-Nuneaton line, Stanier 8F no. 48263 ran through a set of buffer stops and derailed on 16th December 1963. A pair of breakdown cranes have arrived at the scene and just re-railed the engine in front of a small group of spectators. The crane on the right is marked as belonging to Rugby, though the other is not identifiable. No. 48263 was allocated to Nuneaton at this time and returned to service there until June 1966 when transferred to Agecroft. The locomotive was condemned just two months later. Photograph by Neville Simms from the Ranwell Collection courtesy Rail Photoprints.

Opposite below STAFFORD STATION
Stanier's 8F Class locomotives were built with 4,000-gallon tenders. The majority were paired with this type from new until withdrawn, although a small number saw changes in the late 1940s and 1950s. Towards the end of the latter decade, 3,500-gallon tenders from 42 'Jubilee' Class engines were swapped with the 4,000-gallon tenders of the 8Fs. No. 48258 was one chosen to take tender no. 4495 from no. 45563 *Australia* in early 1960. This in turn had been taken from Fowler 'Patriot' no. 5529 *Stephenson* in June 1947 during another round of switches, though was originally coupled to 'Jubilee' no. 5598 *Basutoland* at that time. No. 48258 ran with the tender until 1964 when reverting to the original type. The engine is at Stafford station in 1961 with a northbound freight service. Photograph by A.J.B. Dodd courtesy Rail Photoprints.

Above STOKE SHED

Despite a large number of recently constructed freight locomotives being in service at Nationalisation, BR decided a new design was necessary to haul heavy loads at faster speeds across the country. The result was the Standard Class 9F 2-10-0 which was built in large numbers from 1954 to 1960, when 251 examples were in traffic. No. 92047 was the product of Crewe Works in February 1955 and was allocated to Wellingborough for a brief time before transferred to Bidston depot near Birkenhead. The engine moved to the latter place's locomotive stabling point in February 1963 and was later condemned there in November 1967. No. 92047 is at Stoke shed – minus front numberplate, though this information has been chalked on – during May 1966. Photograph by Charlie Cross from the Gordon Edgar Collection courtesy Rail Photoprints.

Opposite STOKE SHED

View inside the roundhouse at Stoke in 1964. The North Staffordshire Railway erected the building south of Stoke station in 1852 and originally a more substantial roof was provided. The LMSR re-roofed the building in the mid-1930s and thought that protection from the elements was not necessary, leaving much of the interior open. The roundhouse survived in this form until August 1967 when closed to steam. A second straight shed also housed locomotives at Stoke a short distance to the east on the other side of the running lines to the station. This opened in 1872 and was extended several times over the years. Inside the roundhouse – and identifiable – here are: Fowler 4F no. 44048 (minus tender); Fairburn 4P Class 2-6-4T no. 42226; Fairburn 4P Class 2-6-4T no. 42069. Photograph by A.J.B. Dodd courtesy Rail Photoprints.

Above STOKE STATION

The Grand Junction Railway did not serve many of the pottery-producing areas of Staffordshire when opened in the mid-1830s. By the 1840s, local businessmen were eager to change this and several schemes were brought together under the North Staffordshire Railway. The main line of the company was laid from Norton Bridge (leaving the LNWR route near there) and ran to Stafford, Stone, Stoke, Kidsgrove, Congleton and Macclesfield. Stoke had a temporary station for opening in April 1848, though this was soon replaced by a permanent structure. Here, Stanier 8F no. 48452 passes through the station with a short freight train heading south on 4th May 1965, whilst Stanier 2-6-4T no. 42665 is on the left with a local service. Photograph by B.W.L. Brooksbank.

Opposite above STOURBRIDGE JUNCTION STATION

The first station at Stourbridge was opened during 1852 by the Oxford, Worcester & Wolverhampton Railway just to the north of the facility in this image. In 1860, the Stourbridge Railway line ran from the station to Smethwick where a connection was made with the LNWR's Birmingham-Stafford section of the main line. Later, another junction was made with the GWR's Birmingham-Wolverhampton-Shrewsbury route. Finally, the station became the departure point for a short branch to Stourbridge Town station, the bay platform for the service being located behind the station name board here. Stanier 8F no. 48460 has a mineral train at the station on 31st March 1958. Photograph by B.W.L. Brooksbank.

Opposite below STOURBRIDGE JUNCTION SHED

The 3200 'Dukedog' Class 4-4-0s earned this interesting sobriquet from being constructed from parts previously belonging to Dean 3252 or 'Duke' Class 4-4-0s and Dean 3300 or 'Bulldog' Class 4-4-0s; the cylinders, motion and boiler of the aforementioned were paired with frames of the latter group. No. 9028 was assembled from no. 3256 *Guinevere* and no. 3249, originally becoming no. 3228 and later renumbered. The engine is at Stourbridge Junction shed on 20th June 1956. Photograph by Bill Reed.

Above STOURBRIDGE JUNCTION SHED

A large roundhouse shed was established by the GWR at Stourbridge Junction in 1926. This replaced a four-track straight shed from 1870 that was repurposed for railcars. During the war, the latter returned to steam use and both buildings were closed in 1966. A number of years before this event, in 1957, several of the depot's residents are pictured around the turntable inside the roundhouse. On the left is Collett 1400 Class no. 1458, then Collett 5700 0-6-0PT no. 5719, followed by Collett 8750 no. 9636 and Churchward 4300 Class 2-6-0 no. 4326. Photograph by Hugh Ballantyne courtesy Rail Photoprints.

Opposite SUTTON PARK STATION

In the early 1870s, the Wolverhampton, Walsall & Midland Junction Railway promoted a connection between the Birmingham-Derby main line at Water Orton to Walsall where a junction was formed with the Walsall & Wolverhampton Railway. The route opened in 1879, passing through Sutton Coldfield and parkland to the north west, where a station was built for visitors to the area. Sutton Park was well-served by trains from Birmingham, Wolverhampton and Walsall, though in the 1930s the ex-MR Walsall-Wolverhampton line was closed in favour of the LNWR route and direct trains from Wolverhampton were drastically reduced. In the 1950s, services were just a fraction of the pre-war level and Sutton Park station was a casualty of the 'Beeching Axe' in early 1965. Yet, the line remained important for freight traffic and was kept open, which continues to be the case. The 'Severn & Dee' railtour of 26th February 1967 has made a stop at the closed station with Stanier Class 5 no. 44944. Photograph by Tony Martens courtesy John Law.

Above STOURBRIDGE JUNCTION STATION
The Oxford, Worcester & Wolverhampton Railway opened Stourbridge Junction station as Stourbridge in 1852. During the early 1860s a new line was constructed north of the station by the Stourbridge Railway to Old Hill and this was later extended to Smethwick, meeting the GWR's Birmingham-Wolverhampton route. Yet, the 'Junction' portion of the name was not used until a short branch to the town was opened in 1879. A local service is at Stourbridge Junction station with Hawksworth 9400 Class 0-6-0PT no. 8498 on 12th June 1962. Photograph by B.W.L. Brooksbank.

Opposite above STOURBRIDGE JUNCTION STATION
A goods train from Stourbridge Town arrives at Stourbridge Junction station on 24th March 1951. The locomotive is Collett 8750 Class no. 9613, which was a long-term resident at the local depot, being noted there at least from around Nationalisation until withdrawn. No. 9613 was of relatively recent construction, emerging from Swindon Works in September 1945 and was in traffic until October 1965. Photograph by B.W.L. Brooksbank.

Opposite below STOURBRIDGE JUNCTION STATION
Collett 'Hall' Class no. 5959 *Mawley Hall* travels southward through Stourbridge Junction station with a Class C freight on 31st March 1958. Exeter-allocated at this time, the locomotive transferred to Tyseley in October 1959 and was condemned there nearly three years later. Photograph by B.W.L. Brooksbank.

Above TAMWORTH, ALDERS PAPER MILL

Just west of Tamworth, Alders Paper Mill was established in the 19th century, though the factory had to wait until well into the 20th century for a connection to be made with the nearby Trent Valley line between Tamworth and Lichfield. When the line was laid in the late 1920s, the mill bought this locomotive, an Andrew Barclay 0-6-0ST, works no. 1576 built in 1918. Pictured here during the mid-1960s, the engine was scrapped on site at the end of the decade; around this time the rail connection was lifted. Photograph by Bill Reed.

Opposite above STRATFORD-UPON-AVON

Collett 2251 Class 0-6-0 no. 2210 is serviced at Stratford-upon-Avon during the early 1960s. Introduced in 1930, the 2251 Class was conceived as a replacement for older 0-6-0s and batches were completed up to Nationalisation. No. 2210 was amongst ten erected in 1939 and for some time was the last new class member built with a side-window cab as blackout restrictions saw the feature removed on the following engines; these were later installed following the end of hostilities. Photograph courtesy Colour-Rail.

Opposite below STRATFORD-UPON-AVON

An ore train approaches Stratford-upon-Avon behind Collett 5205 Class 2-8-0T no. 5205 during August 1962. The locomotive was Worcester-allocated at this time and was withdrawn from there at the end of 1963. Photograph courtesy Colour-Rail.

Above TAMWORTH, ALDERS PAPER MILL

Shortly after the end of the Second World War, Alders Paper Mill, Tamworth, purchased a second locomotive to assist Andrew Barclay 0-6-0ST no. 1576. This was no. 1340 *Trojan* which had been constructed by the Avonside Engine Co. in 1897. At first, the engine worked for the Newport Dock Co., but later moved around the GWR system, following absorption into the company at Grouping. Withdrawn in 1932, *Trojan* was sold to the coal industry, then Alders Paper Mill in 1947. After the two locomotives became redundant, no. 1340 was purchased for preservation, though a problematic restoration meant the engine only ran for ten years in the early 2000s. At present, *Trojan* is on static display at the Didcot Railway Centre. Photograph by Bill Reed.

Opposite above TAMWORTH

Rebuilt Fowler 'Patriot' Class 4-6-0 no. 45527 *Southport* approaches Tamworth Low Level station with an express from Euston to Llandudno and Holyhead on 22nd September 1961. Photograph by B.W.L. Brooksbank.

Opposite below TAMWORTH LOW LEVEL STATION

A Euston to Manchester express arrives at Tamworth Low Level station around 1960 behind BR Standard Class 'Britannia' Pacific no. 70046 *Anzac*. Photograph courtesy Rail Photoprints.

Above TAMWORTH

In 1860, the LNWR was the first company to pioneer the use of water troughs for collecting water into the tender without stopping. This was done in an effort to save time as part of an improvement of the 'Irish Mail' train and the first set was installed at Mochdre between Chester and Holyhead. Whilst the LNWR increased the number of troughs in use, the idea was slow to be embraced by other companies and not until the turn of the century did the other railways add troughs to their respective networks. One of the Midland Railway's sets was installed just north of Tamworth near the village of Wigginton known as Haselour Troughs. Stanier Class 8F no. 48490 is taking on water there whilst working a coal train during 1963. Photograph by Norman Preedy courtesy Rail Photoprints.

Opposite TAMWORTH

The Birmingham & Derby Junction Railway was the first line to pass through Tamworth when opened in 1839. Before the end of the 1840s, the LNWR's Trent Valley line, which bypassed the congested Birmingham area, crossed over the original route at Tamworth. This resulted in a joint station that later saw the titles High Level and Low Level used to differentiate the two lines – Birmingham to Derby and Birmingham bypass respectively. Stanier Class 5 no. 45407 is at Tamworth on the High Level line with a freight train on 19th April 1963. The locomotive was constructed by Armstrong Whitworth in September 1937 and spent much of the BR period working on ex-Midland Railway lines in the Midlands; by the early 1960s, the engine was allocated to Burton-on-Trent. In March 1965 no. 45407 transferred to Speke Junction and had three months at Lostock Hall before withdrawal in August 1968. Photograph by Geoff Warnes.

Above TYSELEY SHED

The GWR established a major motive power depot near Tyseley station in 1908. Two roundhouses were built, along with a repair shop and other facilities. Inside one of the roundhouses on 31st January 1965 are three non-residents of Tyseley: Stanier Class 8F no. 48351, BR Standard Class 5 no. 73035 and Collett 'Manor' Class no. 7818 *Granville Manor*. The latter was recently withdrawn, whilst no. 73035 was based at Shrewsbury, later moving to Patricroft and surviving until January 1968, and no. 48351 was Saltley-allocated. Tyseley shed was closed in late 1966 and part of the land was purchased to house preserved locomotives, later adapting to perform maintenance and overhauls. Photograph by Richard Postill.

Opposite above TYSELEY SHED

One of the final Collett 'Castle' Class 4-6-0s is at Tyseley shed on 22nd November 1964. Construction of the class had commenced in 1923, with the engines to be used on the GWR's principal expresses. Several further batches were produced at Swindon up to the Second World War, followed by three more after the conflict up to 1950 when 171 had been built. No. 7034 *Ince Castle* was fourth to last in traffic in August 1950 and had a slightly modified boiler from pre-war engines. The locomotive has also been fitted with a double chimney. No. 7034 was withdrawn from Gloucester in June 1965. Photograph by Bill Reed.

Opposite below TYSELEY SHED

Collett 5600 Class 0-6-2T no. 6681 was a recent addition to the ranks at Tyseley shed. Pictured on 22nd November 1964, the engine had arrived two months earlier and was employed for a year, being condemned at the depot in October 1965. Photograph by Bill Reed.

Above TYSELEY SHED

Three of the residents of Tyseley depot stand around one of the turntables in February 1961. On the left is Collett 'Hall' no. 5959 *Mawley Hall*, in the middle is Collett 'Grange' 4-6-0 no. 6861 *Crynant Grange* and right is BR Standard Class 4 no. 75024. No. 6861 had arrived at Tyseley from Oxley in December 1955 and was withdrawn from the former in October 1965. No. 75024 entered traffic in December 1953 and had several allocations before beginning work at Tyseley in September 1959. Moving on to Machynlleth in December 1962, the locomotive survived until November 1967. Photograph by Dave Cobbe courtesy Rail Photoprints.

Opposite UTTOXETER SHED

Uttoxeter was first connected to the rail system in 1848 with the opening of part of the eventual line between Derby and Stoke by the North Staffordshire Railway. With the completion of a temporary station was that of a servicing and stabling point for locomotives. Two years later, a new shed was built and used until the turn of the century. This building was located near Bridge Street station, though two other stations were in use: Uttoxeter Junction between the Stoke-Derby line and route to Macclesfield (opened 1849) and Uttoxeter Dove Bank on the last mentioned line. In 1881 the NSR amalgamated all three into a new station east of Bridge Street station in the western point of the junction between the Stoke-Derby line and the Macclesfield route. The third shed was erected to the east of the new station in 1901 and the building is visible here in the background as Stoke's Stanier 4P Class 2-6-4T no. 42663 is serviced on 29th August 1964. Photograph by Hugh Ballantyne courtesy Rail Photoprints.

Above UPTON-ON-SEVERN STATION

Johnson M (3F) Class 0-6-0 no. 43645 has the 17.45 service to Ashchurch at Upton-on-Severn station on 9th July 1955. The locomotive was one of 345 erected to the design between 1892 and 1902, specifically being the product of Dübs & Co. in April 1900. Originally no. 2566, the engine was renumbered 3645 in August 1907 and was fitted with a type H boiler in May 1915, later receiving a G7 boiler in February 1924. No. 43645 was a long-term servant at Gloucester Barnwood shed and was condemned there in November 1962. Photograph by Hugh Ballantyne courtesy Rail Photoprints.

Opposite above WALSALL STATION

Stanier 8F no. 48254 was built for the War Department by the North British Locomotive Company in July 1941 and towards the end of the year was dispatched for service in Persia. Around Nationalisation, BR and the War Department reached an agreement for surplus locomotives overseas to return to Britain for service in the country. No. 48254 was accepted into stock during December 1949. Interestingly, another War Department 8F had been built earlier by the NBLC and taken on loan by the LMSR, receiving no. 8254 for several months until sent to Persia, later working in Egypt. No. 48254 is at Walsall station on 23rd April 1966 with a train of coal wagons. The engine is coupled to a Fowler 3,500-gallon tender and the pairing with this type lasted from 1958 until withdrawal in August 1966. Photograph by Richard Postill.

Opposite below WALSALL

Beames G2 Class 0-8-0 no. 49430 has partnered with Fowler 4F 0-6-0 no. 44358 to work a freight train from Bromford Bridge during March 1963 and the pair has paused at Walsall. Photograph courtesy Rail Photoprints.

Above WESTMOOR FLAG STATION

North west of Hereford, Ivatt Class 2MT 2-6-0 no. 46506 has the 12.42 service to Three Cocks Junction on 6th June 1960. The train is passing Westmoor Flag station which was operated privately from opening in 1863 and in use for an unknown period, although official closure was at the end of 1962. The building currently survives and has been listed. Photograph by Hugh Ballantyne courtesy Rail Photoprints.

Opposite above WASHWOOD HEATH

Stanier 'Coronation' Class Pacific no. 46235 *City of Birmingham* crosses the ex-Midland Railway lines at Washwood Heath with a train of empty coaching stock in 1957. The Grand Junction Railway curved towards Birmingham just north west of this point and the successor LNWR built a connection, where the locomotive is located, between Aston and Stechford on the former London & Birmingham line in 1880. Photograph courtesy Rail Photoprints.

Opposite below WASHWOOD HEATH

Johnson J2 (2F) Class 0-6-0 no. 58261 is at Washwood Heath with a goods train on 27th April 1957. The Midland Railway first established a marshalling yard in the area during the late 1870s and subsequently added more sidings as traffic grew, with the LMSR continuing to improve facilities up to the 1930s. No. 58261 was a long-term resident of Saltley shed and was withdrawn from the depot in January 1960 after nearly 70 years in service. Photograph by B.W.L. Brooksbank.

Above **WEST BROMWICH STATION**

Nameless BR Standard Class 'Britannia' Pacific no. 70045 (*Lord Rowallan*) has the Saturday only 08.00 service from Wolverhampton to Minehead at West Bromwich station on 26th June 1965. Originally a private enterprise, the Birmingham, Wolverhampton & Dudley Railway was soon taken over by the GWR which used the route as part of the company's expansion northward. Construction came to an end in 1854 and West Bromwich station was one of the stops on the line for opening in mid-November. The line would not have been built if the LNWR had agreed to grant the GWR running powers and the duplication of lines in the area resulted in the closure of the Snow Hill to Wolverhampton route in the early 1970s. Yet, much of the route was adopted for a tramway in the late 1990s and a new station was built on part of the old site. Photograph by Ian Turnbull courtesy Rail Photoprints.

Opposite above **WEDNESBURY STATION**

Hawksworth 'Modified Hall' no. 7915 *Mere Hall* has a short freight train at Wednesbury station on 22nd June 1964. The locomotive entered traffic from Swindon in March 1950 and was in service until October 1965. From November 1962 to the latter date the engine was allocated to Tyseley. Photograph by David Christie.

Opposite below **WELLINGTON (SALOP) STATION**

The 13.10 parcels train from Wellington to Crewe prepares to depart on 28th September 1965 behind 'Manor' Class no. 7821 *Ditcheat Manor*. Photograph by Bill Wright.

Above WELLINGTON (SALOP) STATION

Wellington station was a hub for several lines in the area (east of Shrewsbury). The station was opened in June 1849 as part of the route between Shrewsbury and Wolverhampton, instigated by the Shrewsbury & Birmingham Railway and built jointly with the Shropshire Union Railways & Canal Company. The latter also completed the line from Stafford via Newport around this time. In 1857 the Wellington & Severn Junction Railway joined the main line near Wellington, then ten years later the Wellington & Drayton Railway opened to traffic and connected with the Nantwich & Market Drayton Railway; these two companies later provided the GWR with access to Crewe. Collett 8750 Class 0-6-0PT no. 9639 is at Wellington station c. 1960 with a local service. Built in February 1946, the locomotive was allocated to Wellington soon afterwards and worked there for many years, being transferred to Croes Newydd in September 1964; withdrawal occurred there a year later. Photograph by Bill Reed.

Opposite above WELLINGTON (SALOP) STATION

At first glance Stanier Class 5 no. 44666 has a mixed freight train at Wellington station on 28th September 1965. Looking closer, a nuclear fuel container is coupled behind the tender and part of the train, which is the 03.25 from Carlisle to Stoke Gifford. No. 44666 was coming to the end of an allocation to Saltley shed at this time and unusually for the period has the depot's name painted on the bufferbeam. Photograph by Bill Wright.

Opposite below WELLINGTON (SALOP) STATION

Work-weary 'Manor' Class no. 7821 *Ditcheat Manor* is at Wellington with the 13.10 parcels train to Crewe via Market Drayton on 28th September 1965. Both the nameplate and cabside numberplate have been removed, as has much of the paint on the smokebox thanks to excessive heat. The locomotive had just two months left in service before sent to the scrapyard. Thankfully, this was Woodham Bros and no. 7821 was rescued in 1980 and subsequently restored. At present, *Ditcheat Manor* requires another extensive overhaul and is on display at Swindon Designer Outlet which occupies part of the old works site. Photograph by Bill Wright.

Above WELLINGTON (SALOP) STATION
A southbound express is at Wellington station on 12th June 1962 with 'Castle' no. 5031 *Totnes Castle*. Photograph by Bill Reed.

Below WELLINGTON (SALOP) STATION
Hawksworth 'County' Class no. 1018 *County of Leicester* is ready to proceed with an express from Wellington station on 12th June 1962. Photograph by Bill Reed.

Above WELLINGTON (SALOP) STATION

A local service is at Wellington station on 12th June 1962 with 6400 Class no. 6421. The engine was at Wellington for just a year in the early 1960s. Photograph by Bill Reed.

Below WELLINGTON (SALOP) SHED

Collett 5101 Class no. 4178, 6400 Class no. 6421 and Ivatt Class 2MT 2-6-2T no. 41204 are outside the shed at Wellington on 12th June 1962. Photograph by Bill Reed.

Above WEST CANNOCK NO. 5 COLLIERY
No. 7 *Wimblebury* was new from the Hunslet Engine Co. to Wimblebury Colliery in 1956. In the mid-1960s, the engine had spells at Cannock Central Workshops and Cannock Wood Colliery. From the latter, no. 7 was taken to Foxfield Railway and the engine has recently returned to service after an overhaul. Photograph by Bill Reed.

Opposite above WEST CANNOCK NO. 5 COLLIERY
Located to the north of Hednesford station, West Cannock No. 5 Colliery was one of several owned by the West Cannock Colliery Co. Ltd. Sunk in 1917, coal was mined until 1982. W.G. Bagnall 0-6-0ST *Topham* is at the colliery on 17th May 1971 and had worked at the site for many years, although there had been several spells away at nearby collieries. In 1972 the locomotive was preserved and worked for a time on the Foxfield Railway, though *Topham* is now stored at the Spa Valley Railway. Photograph by Bill Reed.

Opposite below WEST CANNOCK NO. 5 COLLIERY
Hunslet Engine Co. 0-6-0ST no. 8 arrived at West Cannock No. 5 Colliery in early 1971 and worked there for several years, being moved on to Granville Colliery at the end of the decade. Photograph by Bill Reed.

Above WESTON RHYN

An express led by BR Standard Class 5 no. 73014 passes over the level crossing at Weston Rhyn (north of Gobowen, on the ex-Shrewsbury & Chester Railway) on 1st September 1965. No. 73014 was one of 130 class members built – of the total 172 – at Derby Works between April 1951 and June 1957, being sent into traffic during September 1951 to Sheffield Millhouses depot. After several transfers, the engine reached Banbury in June 1965, though moved northward to Bolton in April 1966 and survived a further 15 months before condemned. No. 73014 was part of a small group of Standard Class 5s to be painted in lined green livery during the late 1950s and 1960s, which was at odds with the official standard of lined black for the class. The colour scheme was first applied to no. 73014 at Eastleigh in March 1964 and is now quite obscured by grime accumulated in service. Photograph by David Christie.

Opposite WILMCOTE STATION

Collett 2251 Class 0-6-0 no. 2211 makes a stop at Wilmcote station with a local service from Stratford-upon-Avon on 17th May 1963. The branch from the GWR main line at Hatton to Stratford-upon-Avon had been open for over 100 years at this time, whilst a second route to Birmingham was in use from 1907. This ran northward via Henley-in-Arden to reach the main line at Tyseley. No. 2211 had been in service from May 1940 and would continue in traffic until November 1964. From December 1960 until the latter date, the locomotive was allocated to Leamington Spa. Photograph by Neville Simms from the Ranwell Collection courtesy Rail Photoprints.

Above WOLVERHAMPTON HIGH LEVEL STATION

As the end of steam approached, certain anomalies crept into maintenance practices. One was the lack of lining applied to locomotive liveries and several Stanier 'Jubilee' Class 4-6-0s were pictured with unlined BR green in the 1960s. No. 45675 *Hardy* was one and the engine is at Wolverhampton High Level station in the mid-1960s. For the vast majority of the BR period, the locomotive was employed at Leeds Holbeck shed. Photograph by Bill Reed.

Opposite above WOLVERHAMPTON LOW LEVEL STATION

The 09.10 Paddington to Birkenhead 'Cambrian Coast Express' service was particularly popular after Nationalisation and this resulted in the formation of a relief express during 1950. The 'Inter-City' left Paddington 10 minutes earlier and omitted the stop at Leamington to reach Birmingham at 11.10 and Wolverhampton by 11.35. Unlike the main service, the relief terminated at the latter city and returned to London at 16.25, with arrival scheduled for 19.05. The 'Inter-City' ran until the early 1960s when diesels revolutionised services. 'Castle' Class no. 5032 *Usk Castle* is at the head of the train at Wolverhampton Low Level station on 31st March 1958. Photograph by B.W.L. Brooksbank.

Opposite below WOLVERHAMPTON STAFFORD ROAD SHED

Between Oxley and Wolverhampton Low Level station, the GWR developed a large servicing point near Stafford Road over a number of years, beginning in 1854 with the erection of a three-track building. In 1860, the first roundhouse was erected, followed by two more in 1874 and 1875, as well as further straight sheds in 1864 and 1882. By the mid-1950s, the depot boasted around 60 locomotives in the stud, many being 4-6-0s. In this image, dating from 4th September 1962, several of this type are in the shed yard. From left to right they are: 'Hall' Class no. 5925 *Eastcote Hall*; 'Castle' no. 7006 *Lydford Castle*; 'Castle' no. 7026 *Tenby Hall*; 'Castle' (rebuilt from Churchward 'Star') Class no. 5089 *Westminster Abbey*. Wolverhampton Stafford Road shed was closed in September 1963 and the site repurposed for use by industrial units. Photograph by B.W.L. Brooksbank.

Above WOLVERHAMPTON STAFFORD ROAD

Whilst the eastern side of Stafford Road, Dunstall Park, Wolverhampton, was dedicated to stabling locomotives, the other side housed a locomotive works where a number of engines were erected for the GWR in the early years of the company. Later, Swindon Works was chosen to be the principal site of construction and Wolverhampton Works was left to focus on repairs. The shops had been established by the Shrewsbury & Birmingham Railway in 1849, though initially used for repairs, the first engine was erected in 1859; a further 793 locomotives were built to 1908. Repairs continued, in part thanks to a modernisation of the shops in the mid-1930s, until mid-1964 as part of BR's rationalisation of the workshops division. Collett 5101 Class 2-6-2T no. 4165 has just been refreshed in the workshops during July 1960 and will return to traffic at Gloucester shed. The engine had several transfers subsequently and was condemned at Oxley depot (a short distance from the works site) in October 1965 after more than two years there. Photograph by Ian Turnbull courtesy Rail Photoprints.

Opposite above WOLVERHAMPTON LOW LEVEL STATION

Wolverhampton Low Level station was built in the early 1850s by the GWR, as part of the Birmingham, Wolverhampton & Dudley Railway, and the Oxford, Worcester & Wolverhampton Railway, opening in 1854 as Wolverhampton, with 'Low Level' officially used two years later. The main station building was designed by Sir John Fowler and constructed using blue engineering bricks, which was particularly unique; the platforms were laid out by Isambard Kingdom Brunel. The station was later remodelled during the 1930s owing to the deterioration of the original train shed. Collett 'King' Class 4-6-0 no. 6016 *King Edward V* has a through express at the station during the late 1950s. Photograph by Bill Reed.

Opposite below WOLVERHAMPTON STAFFORD ROAD

'Modified Hall' no. 6964 *Thornbridge Hall* is in the yard at Wolverhampton Stafford Road shed on 20th June 1956. The locomotive was allocated there from November 1953 to July 1957. Photograph by Bill Reed.

Above WOLVERHAMPTON STAFFORD ROAD SHED
Originally constructed as Churchward 3150 Class 2-6-2T no. 3181, this locomotive was later rebuilt under Collett to 3100 Class specifications becoming no. 3102. The engine is at Wolverhampton Stafford Road shed on 1st March 1953 and appears to have been the victim of a rough shunt. Photograph by Bill Reed.

Below WOLVERHAMPTON STAFFORD ROAD SHED
No. 9316 was erected as a variant of Collett's 4300 Class and is still in pristine condition at Wolverhampton Stafford Road shed on 1st March 1953. The locomotive was modified to 4300 specifications in March 1958. Photograph by Bill Reed.

Above WOLVERHAMPTON LOW LEVEL STATION

Two young 'spotters' are perched precariously above the running lines at the south end of Wolverhampton Low Level station during May 1965. They are trying to identify a Stanier Class 5 working a Class C freight, though this proved impossible. The station saw increased traffic during the mid-1960s as the High Level station was modernised as part of electrification. Yet, this was to be the downfall of the Low Level and services were reduced up to closure in 1972. The site has been redeveloped, whilst retaining many original features such at the station frontage. Photograph by Brian Robbins courtesy Rail Photoprints.

WORCESTER SHRUB HILL STATION

A short train forming the 15.10 service from Worcester Shrub Hill station to Paddington begins the journey eastward with 'Castle' no. 5056 *Earl of Powis*, c. 1960. Photograph by Bill Reed.

Above WORCESTER SHED

'Castle' no. 7021 *Haverfordwest Castle* takes on coal at Worcester shed in the early 1960s. The locomotive has Old Oak Common shed's '81A' code on the smokebox door and this allocation lasted from December 1961 to withdrawal in September 1963. Photograph by Bill Reed.

Below WORCESTER SHED

On the ash pits at Worcester shed is 'Castle' no. 5096 *Bridgwater Castle*. The locomotive has a Hawksworth 4,000-gallon tender in place of the original Collett type. Photograph by Bill Reed.

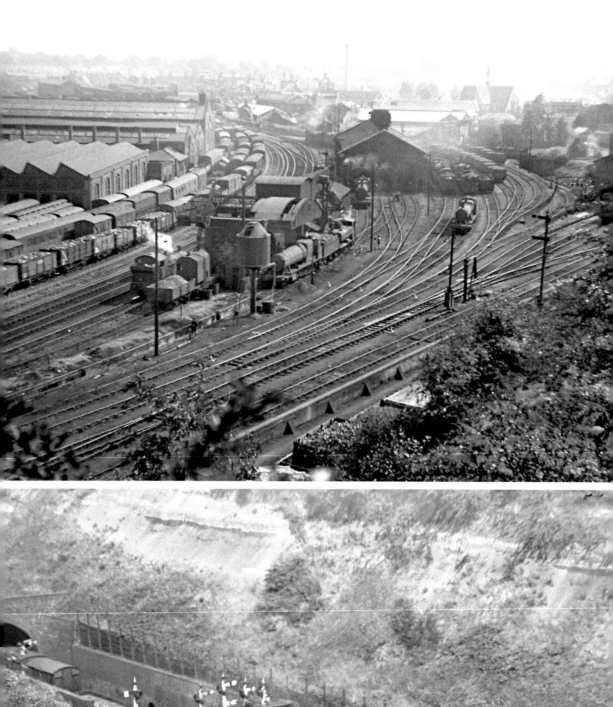

Above WORCESTER WORKS
Founded by the Oxford, Worcester & Wolverhampton Railway, Worcester Works was fully operational until 1952 when tasks were downgraded to heavy repairs only. 'Castle' Class no. 7013 *Bristol Castle* is under the wheel drop, on 12th July 1964, whilst no. 7034 *Ince Castle* is behind and the Hawksworth tender of no. 5042 *Winchester Castle* is on the left. No. 7013 was Tyseley-allocated at this time, though only survived another two months before condemned and no. 7034 was based at Gloucester, lasting until June 1965. No. 5042 was Hereford-allocated, yet at the end of July transferred to Gloucester and was withdrawn in June 1965. Photograph by Hugh Ballantyne courtesy Rail Photoprints.

Opposite above WORCESTER SHED
General view of Worcester shed from Rainbow Hill on 22nd July 1947. The depot was established just north of Shrub Hill station around the mid-19th century and operated as a four-track building – for freight engines, seen extreme right – as well as a three-road structure (centre). The depot was in use until late 1965 when fully transitioned to diesel locomotives. Worcester also possessed a large repair facility and this is present here on the left. Photograph by B.W.L. Brooksbank.

Opposite below WORCESTER RAINBOW HILL
Churchward 4300 Class no. 6324 emerges from Rainbow Hill tunnel, Worcester, with a southbound Class F freight on 22nd July 1947. The locomotive was constructed at Swindon Works in March 1921 and worked until April 1962. No. 6324 had two spells at Worcester depot under BR, with the first lasting from December 1958 to March 1953 and April 1953 to February 1954. Photograph by B.W.L. Brooksbank.

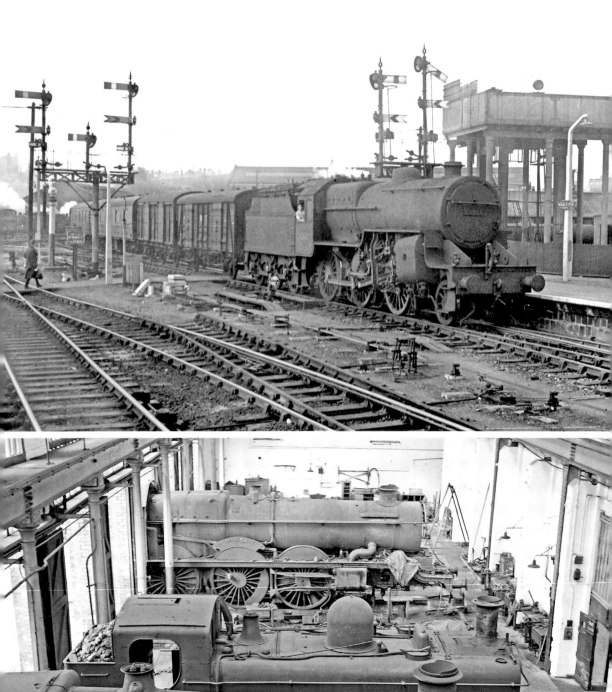

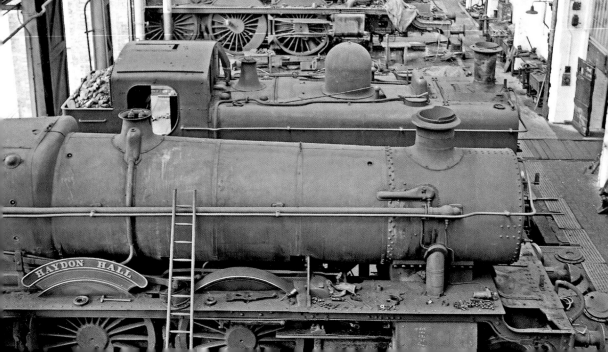

Above WORCESTER SHED
Seventy-five Churchward 4500 Class 2-6-2Ts were erected between 1906 and 1924, with no. 4564 completed at Swindon in October 1924. The class had a mixed traffic designation and had the ability to work on many of the GWR's branch lines. When pictured here at Worcester shed on 20th June 1956, no. 4564 had recently transferred to Gloucester and was allocated there until August 1958. Following moves to Wales and the South West, the locomotive returned to Gloucester in September 1963 and was sent for scrap a year later. Photograph by Bill Reed.

Opposite above WORCESTER SHRUB HILL STATION
The Oxford, Worcester & Wolverhampton Railway and Midland Railway joined forces to open a station at Worcester in 1850, with the latter company arriving via a spur off the Birmingham to Gloucester line. The station was rebuilt in 1865 and in the 1930s remodelling occurred, with the train shed removed. Hughes 'Crab' Class 2-6-0 no. 42839 arrives at Worcester Shrub Hill with a southbound parcels train on 14th April 1959. Photograph by B.W.L. Brooksbank.

Opposite below WORCESTER WORKS
Three engines are inside Worcester Works under attention on 12th July 1964. Closest to camera is Collett 'Hall' Class no. 5932 *Haydon Hall*, behind is Collett 8750 Class 0-6-0PT no. 3683 and in the background stands no. 5042 *Winchester Castle*. No. 5932 was based at Westbury, moving on to Severn Tunnel Junction in August 1964; withdrawal from Bristol Barrow Road occurred in October 1965. No. 3683 was recently allocated to the ranks at Hereford, though the repair did not extend employment beyond October. Photograph by Hugh Ballantyne courtesy Rail Photoprints.

BIBLIOGRAPHY

Allen, C.J. *Titled Trains of Great Britain*. 1983.

Baker, Allan C. *The Book of the Coronation Pacifics Mk2*. 2010.

Christiansen, Rex. *A Regional History of the Railways of Great Britain: Volume 7 West Midlands*. 1983.

Griffiths, Roger and Paul Smith. *The Directory of British Engine Sheds and Principal Locomotive Servicing Points: 1 Southern England, the Midlands, East Anglia and Wales*. 1999.

Griffiths, Roger and Paul Smith. *The Directory of British Engine Sheds and Principal Locomotive Servicing Points: 2 North Midlands, Northern England and Scotland*. 2000.

Haresnape, Brian. *Fowler Locomotives*. 1997.

Haresnape, Brian. *Stanier Locomotives*. 1974.

Hawkins, Chris and George Reeve. *LMS Engine Sheds: Volume Two The Midland Railway*. 1981.

Hunt, David, John Jennison, Fred James and Bob Essery. *LMS Locomotive Profiles: No. 8 – The Class 8F 2-8-0s*. 2005.

Larkin, Edgar. *An Illustrated History of British Railways' Workshops*. 2006.

Quick, Michael. *Railway Passenger Stations in Great Britain: A Chronology*. 2009.

RCTS. *Locomotives of the Great Western Railway Parts 1-12*. 1951-1974.

RCTS. *A Detailed History of British Railways Standard Steam Locomotives: Volume One Background to Standardisation and the Pacific Classes*. 2007.

RCTS. *A Detailed History of British Railways Standard Steam Locomotives Volume Two: The 4-6-0 and 2-6-0 Classes*. 2003.

RCTS. *A Detailed History of British Railways Standard Steam Locomotives: Volume Four The 9F 2-10-0 Class*. 2008.

Shill, R.M. *Industrial Locomotives of South Staffordshire*. 1993.

Summerson, Stephen. *Midland Railway Locomotives Volume Four: Johnson Classes Part II (Goods and Later Passenger Tender Engines), Deeley, Fowler and LTSR Classes*. 2005.

Townsin, Ray. *The Jubilee 4-6-0s*. 2006.

Walmsley, Tony. *Shed by Shed: Part One London Midland*. 2010.

Walmsley, Tony. *Shed by Shed Part Six: Western*. 2009.

Young, John and David Tyreman. *The Hughes and Stanier 2-6-0s*. 2009.

Also available from Great Northern

The Last Years of Yorkshire Steam

The Golden Age of Yorkshire Railways

Gresley's A3s

Peppercorn's Pacifics

London Midland Steam 1948-1966

The Last Years of North East Steam

British Railways Standard Pacifics

Western Steam 1948-1966

The Last Years of North West Steam

Gresley's V2s

Southern Steam 1948-1967

Yorkshire Steam 1948-1967

Gresley's A4s

Gresley's B17s

visit www.*greatnorthernbooks.co.uk* for details.